"A treaty entering the Senate is like a bull going into the arena: no one can say just how or when the final blow will fall, but one thing is certain—it will never leave the arena alive."

John Hay, Secretary of State when he made the above assertion, could scarcely have foreseen how pertinent his trenchant statement would prove following the first World War —and how extremely timely it is apt to be after we are victorious in the present conflict.

Is it not paradoxical that any plans for a just and lasting peace can be blocked by a minority consisting of one-third of the United States Senate? The members of this minority bloc might come from states of small population and might represent only a tiny fraction of the people of this country, yet they would be able to nullify the will of a majority of the voters, of a majority of both Houses of the Congress, and of the Chief Executive.

Professor Colegrove, in this pioneer and hotly controversial book, raises the question whether any minority group should be permitted to retain this power—a question that is vital to world peace and to the future of every one of us.

"A simple, clear, hard-hitting discussion. . . . A brilliant book."—

THE AMERICAN SENATE
AND WORLD PEACE

The

American Senate AND

World Peace

BY KENNETH COLEGROVE

PROFESSOR OF POLITICAL ECONOMY, NORTHWESTERN UNIVERSITY

The Vanguard Press

NEW YORK

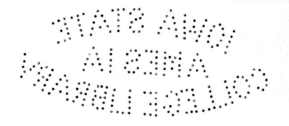

Published for Vanguard Press, Inc., by Pantheon Books, Inc.

Manufactured in the United States of America
by H. Wolff, New York, N. Y.

TO

RALPH BARTON PERRY

CONTENTS

CHAPTER ONE

TREATY-WRECKING HABITS OF THE SENATE

"A treaty entering the Senate," wrote John Hay, "is like a bull going into the arena. No one can say just how or when the final blow will fall. But one thing is certain—it will never leave the arena alive."

These bitter words were penned by America's most brilliant Secretary of State. He had witnessed the heartbreaking defeat of many of his diplomatic achievements at the hands of the United States Senate. The story of these failures is one of the unhappy pages in American history, for John Hay had developed a unique program for the preservation of peace by international agreement. One feature of this plan was the attempt, in 1899 and 1900, to implement the commercial reciprocity policy of President McKinley by negotiating treaties for the reduction of tariff duties with Britain, France, Argentina, and other countries. President McKinley spoke in defense of these treaties in Buffalo on the very day that he was struck down by the hand of an assassin. In spite of the martyrdom of the President, the Senate did not hesitate to assassinate his treaties. Not one of the agreements was approved.

In 1904 and 1905, Hay negotiated a series of arbitration treaties with France, Switzerland, Germany, Portugal, Britain, Italy, Spain, Austria-Hungary, Mexico,

Norway, and Sweden. These treaties were harmless agreements, in which all questions of vital interests, independence, and national honor were exempted from compulsory arbitration. They were another beginning, albeit a modest one, in Hay's project for preserving peace and justice. The Senate, however, viewed these innocuous pacts with such hostility that President Theodore Roosevelt finally withdrew them from its mutilating hands. One motive for opposition to Hay's arbitration treaties was jealous determination to retain every vestige of senatorial power; so much so, that the Rough Rider caustically said: "The individual Senators evidently consider the prerogative of the Senate as far more important than the welfare of the country."

The Open Door policy in China—Hay's greatest diplomatic achievement—was accomplished in 1900 by an exchange of diplomatic notes rather than by a treaty. The resort to this type of international agreement was a deliberate evasion of the treaty-making provision of the Constitution—an evasion sanctioned by President McKinley himself in expectation of Senate opposition to any kind of Open Door guarantee. Hay's victory won the admiration of the world, and evoked grudging praise even from his enemies. In the inimitable language of Henry Adams: "Nothing so meteoric had ever been done in American diplomacy. . . . For a moment, indeed, the world had been struck dumb at seeing Hay put Europe aside and set the Washington Government at the head of civilization so quietly that civilization submitted, by mere instinct of docility, to receive and obey his orders; but, after the first shock of silence, society felt the force of the stroke through its fineness, and burst into almost tumultuous applause. Instantly the diplomacy of the nineteenth century, with all its painful scuffles and struggles was forgotten, and the American blushed to be told of his submissions in the past. History broke in halves."

What handicapped John Hay and what has frustrated many Presidents and Secretaries of State is the provision of the American Constitution providing for the ratification of treaties. Section II of Article II reads: "He [the President] shall have power, by and with the advice and consent of the Senate, to make treaties, provided two-thirds of the Senators present concur." The President thus has power to negotiate treaties, but they can be ratified only with the consent of the Senate. In other words, the solemn confirmation of a treaty negotiated by a President requires the approval of two-thirds of the Senators present at the time the vote on consent to ratification was taken.

Treaties, when duly ratified, become part of the law of the land; according to Article VI of the Constitution, they are on the same footing as acts of Congress. But the enactment of federal statutes requires action by both houses of Congress, and is thus a democratic process; whereas the approval of treaties lies in the hands of the Senate alone and so is an undemocratic process.

The House of Representatives represents the people of the United States. The Senate, as originally established by the Constitution, represented the States rather than the people; but since the Seventeenth Amendment, providing for popular election of Senators, was adopted in 1913, it is more correct to say that the Senate represents the people in each State. Now that both houses represent the people in each Congressional district and in each State, the incongruity of the exaggerated representation of the voters in the small States is all the more apparent. The passage of a federal statute requires a majority vote of both houses of Congress, which now consists of 435 members in the House of Representatives, and 96 members (representing the people in 48 States) in the Senate. New York with a population of 13,479,142 is represented by 43 representatives in the lower house and by two Senators in the upper chamber; Nevada with a population of only 110,247 is represented by one representative and two Senators. The people in both States are represented in proportion to their respective populations in the House of Representatives, but they are each represented by two Senators in the upper chamber. This arrangement gives a disproportionate representation to small States like Nevada.

For historic reasons, this undemocratic system may be tolerated in the process of statute-making. It might even be tolerated for treaty-making, provided the approval of treaties was in the hands of both houses of Congress. But the approval of treaties rests upon a system that is even less democratic than that of statute-making. Only the Senate, with its unequal representation, has the power to ratify international agreements; the House of Representatives, which represents all the people in proportion to population, has no share in the enactment of treaty law. This means that in the making of a treaty (which is as much law as a statute) the State of New York with 13,479,142 inhabitants has only two votes, and Nevada, with only 110,247 persons, also has two votes. In other words, the political power of a single voter in Nevada is equal to that of 120 voters in New York.

The two-thirds rule for treaty ratification has another undemocratic feature. Under the Constitution, the ratification of a treaty requires the "advice and consent" of two-thirds of the Senators present at the session. This provision makes it possible for a minority of the Senators to destroy a Presidential policy which may have the support of two-thirds of the Senators. If the opposing Senators happen to come from the smaller States, it is actually possible for thirty-three Senators representing one-twelfth of the people of the United States to block a treaty supported by sixty-three Senators representing eleven-twelfths of the people. This is the very negation of the democratic process.

Hay's unhappy rebuffs by the Senate were partly due to his failure "to play ball" with Senators who had axes to grind. When, as a young man, he had served as a secretary of President Lincoln, he had become familiar with the game of politics as played in Congress. But his long career in the foreign service, which developed his remarkable skill in diplomatic negotiation, had blunted his capacity for horse-trading with American legislators. He bitterly complained that Senators opposed his treaties for personal, party, or trivial reasons. He was horrified to learn that the votes of members of the upper chamber could be purchased by patronage.

"The fact that a treaty gives to this country a great and lasting advantage," he confided to a friend, "seems to weigh nothing whatever in the minds of about half the Senators. Personal interests, personal spites, and a contingent chance of a petty political advantage are the only motives that cut any ice at present."

"Every day some statesman [Hay's sarcastic reference to Senators] comes up and asks me the true inwardness of the Clayton-Bulwer Treaty," he wrote to Henry Adams, "meaning that if I give him a Consul or two, he will vote for my Treaty next winter." Hay deeply resented the advice of Senator Henry Cabot Lodge to hand out the appointments to legations and consulates in return for votes for his carefully negotiated treaties. To Joseph H. Choate he said: "Now the irreparable mistake of our Constitution puts it into the power of one-third plus one of the Senate to meet with a categorical veto any treaty negotiated by the President, even though it may have the approval of nine-tenths of the people of the nation."

While many of his stinging criticisms of the Senate were well merited, it must be admitted that Hay's inability to cope with the upper chamber was partly the result of his reluctance to play the role of politician. Other Secretaries of State, less skilful in diplomatic negotiation, but more willing to barter patronage for votes on treaties, have enjoyed a larger measure of success in winning Senate approval.

The two-thirds rule for treaty approval has been defended on the ground that it saves the country from harmful treaties—a weak argument, indeed. The rule has saved the United States from no pernicious treaty; it has been the means of rejecting many treaties well designed to promote the best interests of the American people. Minority control of foreign policy is always dangerous. Majorities are seldom protected by minorities; almost invariably the minority, by obstruction, confusion, division, and delay destroys the majority as well as the nation. If simple majorities in both houses of Congress cannot protect the country, the nation is already lost.

The two-thirds rule provokes partisan discussion of foreign policy, but the welfare of the country demands that politics cease at the water's edge. Senators, like Representatives, are politicians; they watch the interests of their political party as avidly as does any member of the lower house.

It is not often that a political party commands a two-thirds majority in either house. More often the President's party has a bare majority. It is thus extremely rare for a treaty to be approved by a two-thirds majority consisting entirely of the President's party. Generally, the opposing party occupies more than one-third of the seats in the Senate. At such times, the opposition party, if party loyalty be enforced, holds the fate of any treaty in its hands. As politicians, many Senators find that they have more to gain by embarrassing the President than by considering the interest of the people.

American diplomatic history shows a long record of

treaties which have been rejected because of partisanship. In 1824, a treaty negotiated with Great Britain for the suppression of the slave trade, although ratified by the Senate, was so mutilated by amendments that the British Government quite properly refused to accept them and the treaty was abandoned. On this occasion, the opposition of the Senators to the treaty seemed to be dictated solely by partisanship. The attack on the treaty was nothing less than a plot to discredit John Quincy Adams, Secretary of State under President Monroe, and also, unluckily, a candidate for the presidency.

Among other victims of politics was the treaty of 1844 for the annexation of Texas. Negotiated while John C. Calhoun presided over the Department of State, this treaty provided for the almost inevitable union of the Lone Star State with our expanding republic. As events demonstrated, the treaty had the support of a large majority of the American people. Nevertheless, in the midst of a presidential campaign it became the football of politics. Most Democrats in the Senate favored the treaty; all but one Whig Senator opposed it. The treaty was defeated by a vote of 16 to 35.

In December, 1844, after the presidential election, President John Tyler deliberately circumvented the Senate by proposing that Congress annex Texas by a joint resolution of the two houses of Congress. The majority in both houses hailed this device as the only satisfactory solution. In the House of Representatives, the resolution of annexation was carried by a vote of 132 to 76, and in the Senate by a vote of 27 to 25.

The annexation of Hawaii followed the same pattern of frustration, evasion of the Constitution, and final accomplishment. In 1897, President McKinley submitted to the Senate a treaty with the Republic of Hawaii providing for annexation. Once again, a two-thirds majority in favor of the treaty could not be mustered in the Senate. Democrats opposed the treaty as a Republican measure and a few isolationist Republicans stood with them. On this occasion, as in 1844, wiser statesmen retrieved American foreign policy by a palpable elusion of the Constitution. On behalf of the President, a joint resolution for annexation was introduced in the House of Representatives. On June 15, 1898, the lower chamber passed the resolution by a vote of 209 to 91, and the Senate, by a vote of 42 to 21. Thirty-six Republicans and six Democrats voted for annexation and nineteen Democrats and two Republicans against it.

The able diplomat, John Foster, bears witness to the fact that although Republican leaders regarded the expedient of a joint resolution for the annexation of Hawaii as a violation of the Constitution and the creation of a bad precedent, they were nevertheless willing to set aside the fundamental law on the ground of national expediency. It is well to ponder the moral justification of this policy while one speculates on the dire consequences of a strict observance of the Constitution. What if Texas had not been annexed? What if the campaign to acquire Hawaii had collapsed?

The Republic of Texas, under the protection of Great Britain and France, would have been a thorn in the side of the United States. "Manifest destiny" in the form of the westward movement demanded the union of Texas with the United States. So also did the aspiration of American pioneers on the expanding frontier—men who desired above all other things to retain their American citizenship while building new homes in the wilderness.

As with Texas, so also with Hawaii. The westward movement, a democratic development of our frontier republic, refused to stop at the Pacific Ocean. Missionary zeal spread American influence into the South Seas, Yankee enterprise sought legitimate trade with the Orient; and Hawaii came within the orbit of American expansion. Geography itself demanded American annexation of the islands, for the strategic archipelago was almost twice as close to the American continent as to the mainland of Asia. In a world of power politics the islands were more naturally a part of the American system than of any Oriental regime. Already Japanese immigration had flooded Oahu. Hawaii, in the hands of Nippon, would have proved a threat to the Open Door Policy in China, and a menace to the defense of San Francisco and Seattle.

In all fairness it must be said that not every treaty defeated by the Senate has been a lost opportunity for the American people. Nor has every defeated treaty been blocked simply because of the two-thirds rule. A case in point is the controversy over the fortification of the Panama Canal. The defeat, in 1900, of the first

Hay-Pauncefote Treaty, which provided that a neutralized Atlantic-Pacific Canal be constructed and managed solely by the United States, was not brought about by the two-thirds rule. The Senate blasted this treaty with three amendments, one of which, unanimously adopted, was intended to correct a serious defect in the treaty, namely, the provision that the Canal was not to be fortified. Two years later, the second Hay-Pauncefote Treaty, placing no restrictions on American defense of the Canal, was ratified by a vote of seventy-two to six. History soon proved that the provision for defense of the Canal was well advised. The era of the Monroe Doctrine and the *Pax Britannica* was on the wane, while the age of totalitarian and global warfare was about to open. Rules of international law, not backed by guns, would have been insufficient to protect the Canal in the new age.

However, most of the admirable policies contained in treaties defeated by the Senate as a result of the two-thirds rule have been supported either by a majority of the Senate or by a majority in both the Senate and the House of Representatives.

The Senate minority has frequently thwarted the aspirations of the American people. It has also contributed to world anarchy by obstructing the progress of international arbitration. We have already seen how the Senate, in 1904, frustrated John Hay's attempt to inaugurate a judicial system. In 1912, it emasculated the arbitration treaties negotiated by President Taft and his Secretary of State, Philander C. Knox. Senatorial opposition to proposals for American support of the Permanent Court of International Justice proved to be a repetition of the same old story. For years, public opinion demanded American entry into the World Court. Peace societies and civic organizations petitioned Congress for adherence to the protocol of the Court. Presidents Harding and Coolidge urged this step. In March, 1925, the House of Representatives supported the proposal by the overwhelming vote of 302 to 28. Stung into action, in 1926 the Senate accepted the protocol, but with amendments regarding the advisory opinions of the Court that empowered the United States, at its discretion, to paralyze the conciliation procedure of the League of Nations. Naturally, the fifty-seven signatory powers of the protocol demurred. Even so, these powers, agreeing that America's support was worth almost any price, proposed a compromise on advisory opinions that conceded almost every demand of the Senate. The compromise had been originated by Elihu Root, an American jurist of outstanding reputation. But the Senate would have none of it.

In 1935, public opinion again forced action upon the Senate. But once more, after a vicious propaganda campaign, the Court was defeated by a vote of fifty-two to thirty-six. As in 1919-1920, when seven votes were lacking for a two-thirds majority in favor of the League of Nations, so also in 1935 only seven votes were missing for a two-thirds majority in favor of the Court. The Court had a simple majority in the Senate. If the two-thirds rule had been abolished previously, the United States would have been able to take its place in the family of nations in support of the only World Court that has ever existed.

The peak of partisan obstruction to the treaty-making objective of the Chief Executive occurred at the end of World War I. The United States had entered the war against Germany as an "Associated" rather than as an "Allied" Power. Nevertheless, this country had conducted hostilities against the Hohenzollern war machine as a power fully allied with Britain and France. The ultimate victory achieved the great purpose of this democracy, namely, "to make the world safe for democracy." Common prudence dictated that the alliance which had won the war should be retained for the purpose of keeping the peace.

It was this policy which guided President Woodrow Wilson at the Paris Peace Conference in 1919. In spite of the obstruction of Lloyd George and of Clemenceau, the American President was able to compel acceptance of a policy of universal co-operation. Whatever the faults of the Treaty of Versailles may have been, it at least had the virtue of attempting to change the alliance of war into a union of peace. It provided for the creation of a permanent and universal peace organization; it assured the means whereby in the future any injustice of the treaty itself might be corrected; it provided a method for collective opposition to international aggressors, and for peaceful change.

Under the astute leadership of Senator Henry Cabot Lodge, the Presidential attempt to secure American participation in the peace system of 1919 was destroyed. On this occasion, as frequently happens, the Covenant of the League of Nations was defeated by a minority. On the final vote on March 19, 1920, the resolution of consent to ratification received 49 affirmative votes and 35 negative ones. This was a majority, but lacked seven votes of the requisite two-thirds majority.

Some have defended the Senate's monopoly of the power to approve treaties. Justice Joseph Story, in his celebrated *Commentaries on the Constitution* (1833), declared that the treaty-making power insured safety and efficiency. This flattering view, however, was expressed before the treaty-wrecking habits of the Senate were fully formed. In 1906, John W. Foster, in his *Practice of Diplomacy*, held that while Senators were partisan on domestic questions, in international relations they were "generally actuated by a high spirit of patriotism." But the account of Senatorial opposition to the treaty for the annexation of Hawaii which Foster gives in his own *Diplomatic Memoirs* contradicts his general statement. In a more recent defense of the Senate, Senator Guy M. Gillette, of Iowa, opposes the sharing of the treaty-making power with the lower house. "The House of Representatives," he says, "is not a continuing body like the Senate, but almost entirely changes its personnel every two years. To make treaties subject to the ratification of this rapidly changing branch would almost assuredly inject these treaties into turmoil and the tender mercies of a political campaign." It is natural for a Senator to consider the Senate less partisan than the House, but most observers are not of this opinion.

The critics of the Senate's monopoly of the approval of treaties constitute a long array of eminent names. Writing in 1884, years before he became President, Woodrow Wilson spoke of the "treaty-marring power" of the Senate. Said Attorney General Wickersham (in the Taft cabinet): "A body of 96 men of such diverse characteristics and opinions as members of the Senate is almost hopeless as an executive force. But it is ideal for the purposes of obstruction."

The most trenchant criticism of the Senate in the annals of our history has perhaps come from *The Nation*. In 1900, during Hay's controversy with the Senate, this weekly used the following language:

The United States is rapidly coming to be regarded by the other great Powers as a nation which is not able to make a treaty. We have been trying to conclude important international agreements during the past fifteen years, but have seen one after another of them go to wreck in the Senate. It is needless to enumerate the long and melancholy list. Whether the President was Cleveland or Harrison or McKinley, whether the negotiators were Democratic or Republican, the power of the Senate to ratify treaties has been mainly exercised as the power to kill treaties. Three valuable conventions with Great Britain have been broken on the Senate's veto. The Chief of State has made treaties with France and Germany, but the Senate has said with a sneer, "They reckon ill who leave me out," and has brought the whole work to the ground. With or without intention, we seem to the world to have stripped ourselves of a leading attribute of sovereignty—the power to make treaties.

John W. Davis, in his presidential address to the American Bar Association, said that it did not "contribute to national influence or prestige or safety that the process of ratifying or rejecting treaties should degenerate into an effort to discover some qualifying formula acceptable to a minority." In a scathing indictment, Dean H. L. McBain, of Columbia University, has branded the Senate's amendment of treaties as international bad manners; and more recently, Senator Joseph H. Ball, of Minnesota, has asserted that the exclusion of the House from treaty-making is undemocratic.

CHAPTER TWO

THE AMERICAN
PEOPLE'S PEACE

THE day is approaching when the last Axis Power will surrender unconditionally. It is none too early to recall the fact that wars generally end with treaties of peace, and that these treaties must be solemnly ratified in accordance with constitutional requirement. But what if one of the victorious allies at the termination of the war is saddled with a process for ratifying treaties which functions badly or not at all? Shall the chief executive of that country attempt to evade the constitution, or shall the country simply stay out of the peace?

This is the problem that confronts the American people. The treaty-making apparatus of the United States is archaic and undemocratic—an eighteenth-century mechanism inadequate to cope with the diplomatic problems of the twentieth century. It has failed the American people on many important occasions; nor can it be relied upon as the means of terminating World War II or of helping to create a peace system which will banish war in the future. It will not insure American participation in the United Nations, although an overwhelming majority of the American people desires such action.

In the summer of 1943, Secretary of State Cordell Hull met several members of the United States Senate in a series of remarkable conferences. The conferees sought to discover a formula for securing Congressional participation in the negotiation of the first reconstruction pact of the United Nations. Some of the conferees looked far into the future. They had visions of finding the pattern for the adoption of all the peace agreements of World War II. In this fashion, they hoped that the United States might be spared the disaster of World War I when America and the Allies won the war only to lose the peace.

The story of the mid-summer conferences has been hinted in the press but never fully told. The account begins with rumors of a plot in the Senate to destroy whatever peace settlement the President might bring forward at the end of World War II. Isolationist Senators, like Burton K. Wheeler, Hiram Johnson, Gerald P. Nye, Robert La Follette, Robert A. Taft, and Arthur H. Vandenberg, had suffered a considerable loss in prestige by the Japanese attack on Pearl Harbor. Millions of citizens realized that if the nation had listened to these prophets of appeasement rather than to President Roosevelt, the United States would have been far less prepared for defense against the sudden assault of the Axis powers. But the isolationists in the Senate have never abandoned hope eventually of weaning America away from active international cooperation. To this end they have counted upon the "inevitable reaction" which they expect at the end of hostilities. When that day finally arrives, they intend to wield a most formidable weapon. This bludgeon is nothing less than the monopoly of the Senate over the approval of treaties together with the two-thirds rule under which a minority of Senators can destroy any treaty negotiated by the President.

Ever since Pearl Harbor, rumors and counter rumors have revolved around the isolationist members of the Senate. According to one account, there have been secret meetings in which the isolationists planned a strategy for annihilating the peace plans of the President. Other rumors insist that there are no clandestine meetings, but rather a man-to-man understanding among these Senators that whenever the Roosevelt-Churchill peace plan reaches the Senate they will spontaneously combine for the destruction of American participation in the United Nations.

Of all departments in the national capital, the Department of State is most susceptible to the effects of rumors. The Department is composed of experts who recall many sad brushes with the Senate. Most of these professional diplomats have an abiding suspicion of the powerful minority entrenched behind the two-thirds rule in the Senate. For the past eleven years, the presiding officer of this Department has been a politico-statesman of conspicuous ability. Cordell Hull served for more than a quarter of a century in Congress before he entered the New Deal cabinet in 1933. Few men are better acquainted with the intricacies of the national legislature. In view of this fact it is significant that the Secretary of State apparently shared many of the suspicions regarding isolationist Senators entertained by his subordinates in the Department. More than this, the astute Secretary has been passionately determined to preserve the presidential postwar policy against all attacks by minority isolationists in the upper chamber.

In the early summer of 1943, isolationist Senators discovered that the Department of State was engaged in negotiating an international agreement for postwar feeding and rehabilitation of devastated countries. It was learned that this pact was to be in the form of an executive agreement, not of a treaty. In other words, the Department of State did not expect to submit it to the Senate for approval. The decision had not been taken without the knowledge of the leadership of both parties in Congress. On June 7, in a conference at the White House, the President had informed the majority and minority leaders of the Senate and the House of Representatives that the first agency of the United Nations would be set up by an executive agreement. Apparently, the leadership of Congress approved this method for keeping postwar peace agencies out of politics. Isolationist Senators, however, were alarmed at this procedure, and soon even supporters of the President's foreign policy became apprehensive.

At the insistence of Senator Arthur H. Vandenberg, of Michigan, the Senate Committee on Foreign Relations considered the problem, and informally disapproved the procedure of the Department of State. A subcommittee of five members was then appointed to confer with the Secretary of State. This subcommittee included the chairman of the Senate Committee, Tom Connally (Texas), together with Elbert D. Thomas (Utah), Theodore Francis Green (Rhode Island), Arthur H. Vandenberg (Michigan) and Robert M. La Follette (Wisconsin).

The subcommittee learned that the Department of State had practically completed negotiations of a relief pact with Great Britain, Soviet Russia, and China, which in turn was to be submitted to the other members of the United Nations for signature. Although simple in design, the pact bore the cumbersome title of the United Nations Relief and Rehabilitation Administration Agreement. Its purpose was to form a joint agency for feeding and clothing the needy peoples of Europe, Africa, and Asia in territories freed from the Axis yoke. Unquestionably, the purpose of the pact had the overwhelming support of the American people.

Challenged by the subcommittee, the Department of State readily agreed to a series of conferences. In fact, the Secretary of State appeared in person. He was accompanied by the American negotiators of the pact, namely, Dean Acheson (Assistant Secretary of State) and Francis B. Sayre (Deputy Director of the Office of Foreign Relief and Rehabilitation Operations). The conferences, however, were far from sugar and sweetness. To his amazement, the Secretary of State found that Democratic Senators, whose support was taken for granted, resented any attempt to ignore the prerogatives of the august upper chamber in which they held membership. In one passage at arms between Cordell Hull and Chairman Connally, the indignant Secretary refused longer to sit with the subcommittee and marched from the room.

Ironically enough, it was Senator Vandenberg who assisted Dean Acheson in mollifying the Secretary and in disciplining the tactless Chairman. In the end, the Department of State accepted radical changes in the text of the agreement demanded by the Senate sub-committee. In return, the subcommittee agreed to recommend to the Senate that the agreement with the United Nations be validated by an act of Congress authorizing appropriations to implement it. This formula, finally evolved by Senator Theodore Francis Green and Assistant-Secretary Francis B. Sayre, on August 24, 1943, promised a happy solution of a much vexed question. Passage of the enabling act would require merely a majority of both houses of Congress and thus would avoid the treaty-wrecking hand of the one-third minority in the upper chamber. At the same time, the use of this procedure afforded the Senate some share in the negotiation of an agreement which otherwise would be entirely in the control of the executive.

State Department officers hoped that the pending agreement might prove to be a pattern for other post-war pacts. If an agreement providing for one agency of the United Nations could be established by virtue of a joint resolution or an enabling act of both houses of Congress, then all agencies of the United Nations might be set up by means of similar pacts. Some officials even hoped that the final peace settlement might take the form of an executive agreement supported by a joint resolution rather than the traditional form of a treaty.

The virtues of the new understanding with Congress were, and still are, obvious. The new formula, if consistently followed, would avoid a disastrous battle between the President and Congress over the method of making the postwar settlement. It would permit Congressional participation in the drafting of the agreements. The defects are also conspicuous. An executive agreement as a substitute for a treaty comes dangerously close to an evasion of the Constitution. The employment of this method would place the postwar pacts on a basis that lacks the traditional validity of treaty-law. It would leave an uncertainty in the minds of our allies who would find American commitments resting on an arrangement which is not expressly defined in the Constitution.

A premature press interview given by Senator Vandenberg to the *New York Times* caused the advocates of a progressive postwar policy to believe that the veteran Senator from Michigan would lead the Republican minority in the direction of international cooperation. In due time, however, Senator Vandenberg showed his true colors. At the Republican Postwar Advisory Council, held at Mackinac Island, he played the leading role in drafting the recommendations on foreign policy. The occasion offered an unrivalled opportunity for inspired statesmanship. But the inspiration was lacking. Wendell Willkie, the foremost Republican advocate of internationalism, and the titular leader of the Republican party, had been carefully excluded from the conference.

A bombshell was thrown into the Mackinac Conference by Governor Thomas E. Dewey who proposed a postwar alliance with Britain. Through Senator Vandenberg's suave management, however, this positive recommendation was effectively buried. Instead of offering a forthright platform for American participation in international co-operation, the Mackinac Declaration straddled this vital issue. In place of a frank advocacy of an alliance with Britain or participation in an international police force to keep the peace, the Declaration merely proposed participation by the United States in some sort of co-operative organization among sovereign nations to prevent military aggression. These weasel words would mean all things to all men. If adopted as the Republican platform in 1944, they would permit isolationists as well as internationalists to rally to the party. The praise which the Declaration immediately won from several isolationists in the Senate gave weight to the belief that it might well serve as the cloak for Senators who plotted to destroy the peace system desired by the American people.

The most damaging part of the Declaration, however, was a proviso specifically intended to wreck the Roosevelt-Churchill peace policy. This provision ran: "Constitutionalism should be adhered to in determining the substance of our policies and shall be followed in ways and means of making international commitments."

By "constitutionalism," the Michigan Senator meant: *The President must be compelled to frame the peace settlement in the form of a treaty, which must*

*be submitted to the Senate, where a one-third minority
of isolationists will be able to destroy it as effectively
as Senator Lodge and his collaborators annihilated
American participation in the peace system at the end
of the First World War.*

The Vandenberg formula of *constitutionalism* has
become the magic weapon of opponents of a postwar
peace system. Rallying around this symbol of defeat-
ism, the isolationists in the House of Representatives
tricked the majority into accepting *constitutionalism*
as a part of the Fulbright concurrent resolution calling
for American participation in postwar international
machinery. The resolution, when pressed to a vote
on September 21, 1943, won 360 ayes. But even with
the devitalizing amendment, 29 isolationists in the
House voted against it, and 41 members refrained
from any vote. To astute observers, all of this appeared
to be but further evidence of a plot to torpedo the
peace settlement at the end of the war.

In the autumn of 1943, as the invasion of Italy
brought the war nearer to its end, there was un-
deniable evidence that the American people desired
to participate in a permanent United Nations to keep
the peace, in an international police force, and in a
military alliance with Great Britain. At the same time,
there was reason to believe that a considerable section
of their representatives in Congress intended to block
these aspirations.

In view of these facts it has become imperative to
ask whether this republic should tolerate the defeat of
the popular will by a minority in the Senate. If this

threat to democratic rule is to be forestalled, several questions must be answered. Is it possible by amendment of the Constitution to secure a democratic procedure in treaty-making? Can this nation escape from the blight of minority control? Is it possible to prevent a plot by a group of clever Senators to thwart the will of the majority of the people?

In the following pages, the problem of constitutional reform of the treaty-making process will be discussed. In approaching the subject it is vital to ascertain the foreign policy which the American people desire to pursue. Then we may ask: Is the treaty-making process under the Constitution adequate for the performance of this policy? If not adequate, what are the means for improvement of this procedure?

The American people have abandoned their policy of isolation. Like many another momentous decision, this change was made with the greatest reluctance. This is nothing new in American history. John Quincy Adams, in explaining the adoption of the Constitution of 1787, declared that it "had been extorted from the grinding necessity of a reluctant nation." He meant that the collapse of the Congress of the Confederation, the disruption of commerce, Shay's rebellion in Massachusetts, and the threat of a tariff war between New York and Connecticut had compelled Washington, Hamilton, Madison, and other leaders to devise a new form of government which was accepted only with the greatest reluctance by the thirteen independent States. The Constitution which the founders of the Republic adopted was built upon the grim experience of the

American people. It was palatable to few, but it was accepted in order to avoid evils less endurable than the form of government that it imposed.

A parallel in historical sequence can be found in the origin of the United Nations. This association of liberty-loving states has come into being in an era even more chaotic than that of the formation of the American Union. The grinding necessity of the twentieth century which is leading the United States reluctantly to become one of the leaders in the movement to create a new peace system is nothing less than the collapse of all devices to eliminate war. Stark reality has convinced the American people that they will be faced with the necessity of waging a new war almost every generation unless by their ingenuity, resources, and force of character they can help to evolve a system for the maintenance of permanent peace.

The American people would prefer to develop their share of this continent without mingling in the affairs of Europe, Asia, and Africa. But the social dynamics of this age have decreed differently. That "no nation liveth unto itself" is even more of a reality in the twentieth century than twenty-six hundred years ago. In a world wherein aggression takes on totalitarian and global form, no state, however great, can avoid becoming involved in power politics. Nor can it remain free from the consequences of a New Order in a Europe dominated by Nazi Germany, or a New Order in a Greater East Asia ruled by the military clique of Japan. Bitter experience is driving the American people to abandon isolation and to participate in the creation of a co-operative peace system.

Our reliance upon isolation as a peace policy has been an unhappy story. Four times, this Republic has been confronted by a world war. Four times, the American people and their government deliberately determined to keep war out of America by resorting to isolation, and every time this attempt has failed. In 1793, after war between Revolutionary France and Austria had broken out, President Washington and his cabinet chose isolation implemented by a policy of neutrality as the means of avoiding war. The policy met defeat, for in 1798 seizures of American shipping led us into a naval war with France. Again, in 1805, after the outbreak of the Napoleonic Wars, we relied upon neutrality, only to enter the War of 1812 through the pressure of world events.

A third time, at the outbreak of World War I in 1914, we put our trust in neutrality. President Wilson went so far as to implore his countrymen to remain neutral even in their thoughts. This time, too, the policy of neutrality proved to be a broken reed. The end of the story approached in the year 1935, when Congress, in anticipation of World War II, revamped our neutrality legislation. We even attempted to appease the militaristic government of Nippon. But the effort to keep the war out of American territory by a policy of neutrality and appeasement was once more doomed to failure, for on December 7, 1941, the Japanese air force attacked Pearl Harbor, while Hitler and Mussolini immediately joined in the declaration of war against the United States.

If the tragic events of the past twenty years prove anything, it is the utter futility of a policy of neutrality and appeasement as a means of maintaining peace. In an age of totalitarian dictatorships that entertain no respect for international law, neutrality simply makes it easier for a *Führer* conveniently to pick off his victims, one by one. This process continued until finally even the Americas were threatened, in spite of their separation from Europe and Asia by two great oceans.

The First World War interrupted the peaceful development of the American nation. It cost the lives of American youth, and it wasted national treasure that might have been devoted to great social enterprises. Now, a generation later, the Second World War has again interrupted our national progress. It has already cost us the lives of thousands of young men, and will saddle us with an enormous national debt. Impressed by these hard facts, the American people are determined, at least at the moment, that this scourge of civilization must cease. As in the case of the adoption of the Constitution of 1787, this great decision has been forced upon a reluctant nation by grinding necessity.

There can be little doubt as to what the American people think about the new peace policy. Reliable public opinion surveys show how fully the citizens of the United States have accepted the necessity for American participation in the creation of a peace system in the postwar world. For instance, in May, 1943, the

American Institute of Public Opinion, commonly called the Gallup Poll, posed the question: "Should the countries fighting the Axis set up an international police force after the war is over to try to keep peace throughout the world?" From the replies it appeared that 74 per cent of the American people favored this policy; only 14 per cent opposed it, and only 12 per cent expressed no opinion. A Gallup Poll in June, 1943, which asked: "Should America play an active part in postwar affairs?" showed the following response:

	TAKE ACTIVE PART	STAY OUT	UNDECIDED
New England	81%	9%	10%
Pacific Coast	80	12	8
Mountain States	79	11	10
Western States	78	13	9
South	76	11	13
Middle Atlantic	76	15	9
Eastern Central	71	18	11

It therefore appears that the voters who want the country to return to the prewar status and remain aloof from international participation constitute a small if somewhat loud minority. The overwhelming majority of the people wish this country to play a new role in world government.

The rapid march of public opinion in most States of the Union is shown in two surveys conducted by *Fortune*. In December, 1941, the question was asked: "After the war, do you think the U. S. should play (1) a larger part, (2) about the same part, or (3) a smaller part in world affairs?" Of the replies received, 58.4

per cent demanded that this country play a larger part in world affairs; the same part, 18.3 per cent; a smaller part, 10.1 per cent; and 13.2 per cent did not know. The same question, asked in June, 1943, elicited a demand for a larger part in world affairs by 76.6 per cent; the same part, by 12.1 per cent; a smaller part, by only 4 per cent; while 7.3 per cent did not know. On this basis, more than three-fourths of the American people demand the complete abandonment of isolation.

Doubts as to the accuracy of the Gallup Poll have been expressed by several isolationist Senators. But their charges have been based on misrepresentation. Neither the Gallup Poll nor the *Fortune* surveys can be compared to the misleading surveys of public opinion on foreign affairs which were conducted by *The Chicago Tribune* and by Representative Hamilton Fish in the two years preceding Pearl Harbor. Both the Gallup and *Fortune* polls are made according to rules formulated by scientific study of the process of sampling public opinion. The accuracy with which these surveys have reflected public opinion on the eve of various elections is concrete evidence of their approximate accuracy. In view of these facts, one can accept the findings of these public opinion surveys as true reflections of what the people are thinking.

There is other abundant evidence of American approval of international co-operation. On March 26, 1943, the Assembly and the Senate of New York adopted a resolution calling upon the President and Congress to lend every effort to the creation of an international organization of all nations to maintain peace. In May, 1943, the legislature of Alabama, by joint resolution, urged the Senate to approve immediate negotiations to create an organization of the United Nations. The immense popularity of Wendell Willkie's *One World* shows the direction of people's thinking. News commentators, editorials in newspapers, letters from readers of newspapers, resolutions of churches and labor unions, all join the refrain in support of American participation in a new peace policy for the postwar world.

This growing public opinion in favor of international co-operation has not gone so far as to favor American entrance into a federal union of democracies, such as is proposed by Clarence Streit. It is probable that this generation of the American people will never approve the surrender of national sovereignty demanded by universal federation. But all evidence now indicates that the American people want their government at least to participate in the maintenance of an international police force and the establishment of a new peace program within the system of states.

It is unlikely that the American people would be content to see their government enter any peace system without assuming a leading role. For the United States, the most powerful combination of people, natural resources and technology in the history of the human race, to take a back seat in the international forum would be both unreasonable and undignified. It is also to the interest of America to assume leadership in the United Nations, for leaders can choose between alternatives, while nations lacking a positive policy simply must take what comes to them.

Happily, the democracies and their allies in the contest with totalitarian dictatorships have made far more progress toward winning the peace while the Second World War is being waged than was ever made in the midst of the First World War. The integration of the war effort by the two foremost democracies (the United States and Great Britain) far surpasses their military co-operation in the war against the Hohenzollern dynasty. Neither Combined Chiefs of Staff nor conferences of the President and the Prime Minister then directed the global war. No agreement had been reached for collaboration upon a new world charter at the end of the war. All these facts create a tendency toward greater integration of political effort when Nazi and Japanese aggression has at last been destroyed.

As early as August, 1941, nearly five months before the United States became an actual belligerent, British and American peace aims were stated in the Atlantic Charter. On January 1, 1942, when the United Nations were created, this Charter became the fundamental agreement of twenty-six powers, including Soviet Russia and China. The Declaration of the United Nations on this occasion was a pledge not only that the struggle will be continued until the final destruction of Nazi tyranny, but also that all would collaborate loyally in the establishment of a new world system.

Since the signing of the Declaration of the United Nations, six other states have adhered to this agreement, making a total of thirty-two states committed to a policy of collaboration for maintaining the monopoly of weapons and the establishment of justice and economic opportunity promised by the Atlantic Charter. In 1919, President Wilson was compelled to wage a desperate struggle to set up a league of nations simultaneously with the termination of the war. In the present war, the United Nations have come into existence even while the war is in progress.

The details of the master plan for peace now being framed by President Roosevelt and Prime Minister Churchill have not yet been fully divulged. The broad outlines of the pattern, however, have been sketched in various addresses to their peoples. Soviet Russia and China undoubtedly will be drawn into the counsels of the master planners as rapidly as possible. Undoubtedly, the United Nations will collaborate in the maintenance of an international police force for many years to come. Some agencies of international control have already been created, and many others will surely be established even before the final peace settlement is negotiated. It is not unlikely that the supreme policy-forming organ will be a United Council, in which the influence of the Big Four—the United States, Britain, Soviet Russia, and China—will prevail, at least for the immediate future. Undoubtedly, the states system will be retained, with no surrender of national sovereignty to the United Council. Federation, or at least confederation, of the smaller states will be encouraged, in order to reduce economic rivalry and to give these states more adequate representation in the United Council.

The Atlantic Charter, to which the United Nations are pledged, calls for economic and social reforms of far-reaching character. All states, great and small, shall have access to international trade and to the raw materials of the world. There shall be collaboration in the economic field so as to secure for all states improved labor standards, economic advancement, and social security. Men in all lands are to live out their lives in freedom from want and fear. All of this is to be undertaken on the assumption that unemployment, starvation, and mass desperation in any country is a menace to world peace. Economic chaos and frustration in any part of the world has become an international as well as a national problem.

The United Nations are pledged to moderate or at least mitigate the evils of the business cycle which almost periodically swings countries from prosperity to depression and back again. What plans are to be followed? What devices are to be employed to guard against destroying the independence of member states or placing an intolerable burden upon the more prosperous states? Obviously, the closest kind of collaboration will be required if headway is to be made in this modern approach to the peace problem. The political questions involved in the maintenance of an international police force, the government of strategic air and naval bases, and the regulation of international mandates in Asia and elsewhere will call for new techniques in international co-operation. But the fulfillment of

the economic and social obligations of the Atlantic
Charter will require a still closer integration of effort.
Reason as well as experience demands these things as
the price of peace. The task is colossal, but it will be
an evil day when the United Nations abandon these
peace aims.

The maintenance of a foreign policy requires commitments or understandings which may, if all other
plans fail, require resort to armed force. In this respect,
isolation and neutrality are not, in the last analysis,
foreign policies. They stop at the water's edge, and
breed a hermit nation.

A foreign policy is positive and dynamic. As Walter
Lippmann has clearly shown in his *U. S. Foreign Policy: Shield of the Republic,* foreign policy reaches its
maximum efficiency when the nation establishes an
equilibrium between its commitments and its resources of power. The minimum commitment that a
state can assume is its own physical defense. But in a
world of global and totalitarian warfare, few states,
perhaps no state, can meet even this commitment without the assistance of other states. In turn, this assistance cannot be assured without alliances and guarantees which entail still further commitments.

For the United States, this means that the very defense of this country depends upon commitments that
extend beyond continental America. In the nineteenth
century, the Monroe Doctrine and British naval supremacy acted like an informal understanding, if not
alliance, that brought a large measure of security to the
United States, the British Empire, and all of Latin

America. But the hegemony of Germany, the growth of Japanese militarism, and the rapid development of Soviet Russia has rendered obsolete the old system of American-British defense.

In the twentieth century, the United States can only be defended by an alliance, as well as membership in a peace system with law-abiding states. Its membership, moreover, must be active not passive. No member of an effective alliance and peace system can expect to escape the responsibility of giving and accepting commitments backed by force. In its own defense, the United States will have to assume mutual commitments, no matter whether we operate within the Big Three (the United States, Great Britain, and Soviet Russia), or the Big Four (the United States, Great Britain, Soviet Russia, and China), or the entire United Nations.

The maintenance of an international police force requires promises from various states regarding the contribution of personnel and war equipment. Persuasion of our own allies, such as Soviet Russia and China, to refrain from the forceful seizure of neighboring lands in Europe and Asia as a means of maintaining their own defense, will needs be purchased at the price of commitments by Britain and the United States. International currency stabilization will necessitate pledges of a financial nature. The opening of the channels of foreign trade will call for economic promises which will be closely related to our political and military commitments.

Commitments, as we have seen, are the essence of

any effective peace system. But most Americans are un-aware of the doubts which other countries have as to the good faith of the United States in the matter of international commitments. Ignorance of the existence of these apprehensions in no sense diminishes their harm to international co-operation. Most of these doubts stem from the abandonment of the peace system of 1919. Naturally, our associates in World War I, when negotiating the Peace Treaty, were aware of the peculiarities of the American Constitution. But, at the Paris Peace Conference of 1919, momentous decisions, involving compromise and sacrifice, could not wait upon the constitutional peculiarities of any signatory power. It was imperative to assume that every state would loyally stand behind the commitments made by its fully accredited representatives. Thus, while there was no legal obligation to ratify the peace system of 1919, there was a moral obligation which was stronger than legal bonds. The repudiation of this moral responsibility by the United States was one of the most profound shocks that the family of nations has ever sustained.

The ghost of the American desertion still stalks the foreign offices of our allies in the present war. If a peace system is to be maintained in the future, commitments must be made by every member of the United Nations, not excepting the United States. But will America accept and fulfill her share of responsibilities in the confederation of peace-loving states? This question worries every one of our allies.

An unanswered doubt is present in every decision

taken by the British cabinet. Should the British Empire rely upon American assistance in the maintenance of a universal peace system? Or should the Empire, in anticipation of another American desertion, now seek to create a new balance of power both in Europe and in the Far East? The same question confronts Dictator Stalin. Is it wise for Soviet Russia to trust that an American-British-Russian understanding will keep Germany from another invasion of the Ukraine? Or is it wiser to put no trust in international security and to extend Russian boundaries beyond the Baltic states, Poland, and even Rumania as the only means of safeguarding the peace of Soviet Russia? The peace of Europe in the next two decades hangs on Russia's answer to these questions.

Almost identical questions confuse our most patient ally, Generalissimo Chiang Kai-shek and the Chungking Government. The same doubts confuse Frenchmen who are striving for the Fourth Republic. Even our Latin American neighbors are perplexed and troubled.

Obviously, the efficacy of American leadership in the United Nations is impaired by the skepticism of the nations that would like to trust us, but still doubt us. Eventually these misgivings may destroy the very fabric of the United Nations. Our allies have scanned with some dismay the Congressional election of 1942, when the Democratic Party lost thirty-four seats in the House of Representatives and eight seats in the Senate. This decline in political strength of the Democratic Party was reminiscent of the defeat of Woodrow Wilson in the Congressional election of 1918. If the Roosevelt administration is on the decline and if Congress is in conflict with the President, of what value are American commitments? If the Republican Party, on accession to office, will reverse all policies of the previous administration simply for the sake of partisanship, and if the Democratic Party, when out of power, will oppose the peace efforts of the Republican Party simply for the sake of opposition, what dependence can be put on American commitments?

Our allies in the United Nations would be neglecting their own self-interest if they failed to ponder these questions. As long as treaties negotiated by our representatives can be upset by any undemocratic minority in the Senate, American commitments must always be subject to discount. Our eighteenth-century treatymaking process fails to meet the needs of the position which we desire to hold in a twentieth century world. Constitutional reform thus seems imperative.

CHAPTER THREE

EVERY SENATOR WANTS TO BE PRESIDENT

THE American people are deeply devoted to the principle of democracy. It is true that there are American Fascists; and there are those who believe in government by the elite. But most Americans, like Lincoln, desire a "government of the people, by the people and for the people."

In our use of the words *democracy*, as well as *democratic process*, there should be no disagreement upon the basic definition of these terms. In its fundamental meaning, democracy (in accordance with the Greek origin of the word) means nothing else than *rule by the people*. Mathematically expressed, this definition connotes government by the majority, namely, one-half plus one or more of the citizens residing within a political unit. Other ideas which we associate with American, British, or French democracy are better designated as assumptions of democracy. Among the assumptions of American democracy are respect for the innate dignity of mankind, freedom of speech, freedom of the press, freedom of religion, the right of opposition parties to exist, and the right of labor to share in the wealth of the nation.

The democratic process, then, simply means that government will express in action the will of the majority of the people, without obstruction by a minority. Measured in these terms, the exclusion of the House of Representatives from the treaty-making power is undemocratic. By the same token, the two-thirds rule in the Senate is the very negation of the democratic process.

"To give a minority a negative upon the majority (which is always the case where more than a majority is requisite to a decision), is, in its tendency, to subject the sense of the greater number to that of the lesser." These are the words of Alexander Hamilton in the twenty-second essay of the justly celebrated *Federalist*. In his defense of the proposed Constitution, Hamilton congratulated his readers that the Senate would remain free from minority rule. It would avoid the helplessness of the historic Polish Diet and the futility of the Congress of the Confederation, whose proceedings had been halted on occasion by the obstruction of only two small States.

Hamilton's hopes that the Senate would never become the victim of minority rule were not realized. This fact, however, does not detract from the validity of his argument for eliminating this impediment to democratic government. In flawless language, Hamilton went on to say:

The necessity of unanimity in public bodies, or of something approaching towards it, has been founded upon a supposition that it would contribute to security. But its real operation is to embarrass the administration, to destroy the energy of government, and to substitute the pleasure, caprice or artifices of an insignificant, turbulent or corrupt junto, to the regular deliberations and decisions of a respectable majority. In those emergencies of a nation, in which the goodness or badness, the weakness or strength of its government, is of the greatest importance, there is commonly a necessity for action. The public business must, in some way or other, go forward. If a pertinacious minority can control the opinion of a majority, respecting the best mode of conducting it, the majority, in order that something may be done, must conform to the views of the minority; and thus the sense of the smaller number will overrule that of the greater, and give tone to the national proceedings.

Appeasement of the minority, according to Hamilton, impairs the operation of government and is detrimental to public welfare. Minority control means, he said:

. . . tedious delays; continual negotiation and intrigue; contemptible compromises of the public good. And yet, in such a system it is even happy when such compromises can take place: for upon some occasions things will not admit of accommodation; and then the measures of government must be injuriously suspended, or fatally defeated. It is often, by the impracticability of obtaining the concurrence of the necessary number of votes, kept in a state of inaction. Its situation must always savor of weakness, sometimes border upon anarchy.

These classic phrases can be applied to the Senate throughout a large part of its history. In the realm of treaty-making, well-planned presidential policies, even during great emergencies, have been rejected, the public will has been flouted, and the animosities and selfish interests of minorities have been imposed upon the nation.

Under the present system of the two-thirds majority the mathematics of minority rule are nothing less than startling. Let us suppose that at the end of a war the President submits a treaty of peace to the Senate. Let us further suppose that the two Senators from New York are in favor of the treaty while one Senator from Nevada opposes it. The vote of the one Senator from Nevada, representing only 110,247 people, under the present system carries as much weight as the vote of the two Senators from New York representing 13,-479,142 people. Now, if the two Senators from Pennsylvania, representing 9,900,180 persons, also approve the treaty, while the second Senator from Nevada opposes it, the two Nevada votes cancel out the four votes of New York and Pennsylvania. In other words, the will of 110,247 persons, as represented by two Senators, successfully overrides the will of 23,379,322. Not all the eloquence in Christendom can prove that this is a democratic process.

Of course, this astonishing incongruity is most apparent when the two extremes in the list of States are used as examples. But we have fourteen States with less than one million inhabitants, and twenty-three States with more than two million. Consequently, the voters in fourteen States have twice as much power as the voters in many other States. And when the two-thirds rule is applied in the Senate, they have four times as much power, for the vote of one Senator against a treaty renders impotent the votes of two Senators in favor of a treaty.

The votes of seventeen States are sufficient to wreck a treaty under the existing rule. If all the votes opposing a treaty should come from the small States, the Senators representing 10,518,249 people would be able to block the will of the 121,151,026 people who live in the largest thirty-one States. In other words, one-twelfth of the American people can prevent eleven-twelfths of the American people from following a course of action in foreign relations.

The undemocratic character of the two-thirds rule can be expressed in even more astonishing figures. Article I, section 5, of the Constitution provides that a majority of the members of each House shall constitute a quorum to do business. A quorum therefore means one-half plus one of the total members of each House, or, in the Senate, forty-nine members. If a bare quorum of the Senate is present when the vote on a treaty is taken, any seventeen Senators can defeat the treaty. If the seventeen negative votes come from the nine smallest States, the obstructionists in the Senate represent only 3,584,511 people out of a total population of 131,669,275. If the thirty-two Senators in the quorum who were in favor of the treaty come from the sixteen largest States, they represent 88,046,234 people. In other words, the will of at least 88,000,000 people can be set aside by that of 3,584,511 people.

POPULATIONS OF THE LARGE AND SMALL STATES

According to the Census of 1940

Seventeen Small States		*Thirty-one Large States*	
1. Arizona	499,261	1. Alabama	2,932,961
2. Colorado	1,123,296	2. Arkansas	1,949,387
3. Delaware	266,505	3. California	6,907,387
4. Idaho	524,873	4. Connecticut	1,709,242
5. Maine	847,226	5. Florida	1,897,414
6. Montana	559,456	6. Georgia	3,123,723
7. Nebraska	1,315,834	7. Illinois	7,897,241
8. Nevada	110,247	8. Indiana	3,427,796
9. New Hampshire	491,524	9. Iowa	2,538,268
10. New Mexico	531,818	10. Kansas	1,801,028
11. North Dakota	641,935	11. Kentucky	2,845,627
12. Oregon	1,089,684	12. Louisiana	2,363,880
13. Rhode Island	713,346	13. Maryland	1,821,244
14. South Dakota	642,961	14. Massachusetts	4,316,721
15. Utah	550,310	15. Michigan	5,256,106
16. Vermont	359,231	16. Minnesota	2,792,300
17. Wyoming	250,742	17. Mississippi	2,183,796
		18. Missouri	3,784,664
Total	10,518,249	19. New Jersey	4,160,165
		20. New York	13,479,142
		21. North Carolina	3,571,623
		22. Ohio	6,907,612
		23. Oklahoma	2,336,434
		24. Pennsylvania	9,900,180
		25. South Carolina	1,899,804
		26. Tennessee	2,915,841
		27. Texas	6,414,824
		28. Virginia	2,677,773
		29. Washington	1,736,191
		30. West Virginia	1,901,974
		31. Wisconsin	3,137,587
		Total	120,487,935

The alignment of votes in the Senate may never occur in this extreme form. But under constitutional law, as it stands today, such a combination is possible;

indeed, is even likely, as long as the two-thirds rule is retained.

THE NINE SMALLEST AND THE SIXTEEN LARGEST STATES

According to the Census of 1940

1. Nevada	110,247	1. New York	13,479,142
2. Wyoming	250,742	2. Pennsylvania	9,900,180
3. Delaware	266,505	3. Illinois	7,897,241
4. Vermont	359,231	4. Ohio	6,907,612
5. New Hampshire	491,524	5. California	6,907,387
6. Arizona	499,261	6. Texas	6,414,824
7. Idaho	524,873	7. Michigan	5,256,101
8. New Mexico	531,818	8. Massachusetts	4,316,721
9. Utah	550,310	9. New Jersey	4,160,165
		10. Missouri	3,784,664
Total	3,584,511	11. North Carolina	3,571,623
		12. Indiana	3,427,796
		13. Wisconsin	3,137,587
		14. Georgia	3,123,723
		15. Tennessee	2,915,841
		16. Kentucky	2,845,627
		Total	88,046,234

Senators, like all men, suffer from many of the frailties of human nature. The Senate, as an organ of government, shares power with the President, which has led some Senators to think that they share this power personally with the Chief Executive. The small size of the Senate as compared with the House, and the Senate's authority to approve treaties and to confirm the President's nominations have given Senators a prestige far beyond that of Representatives. The Senate has proved to be a fertile breeding ground for Presidential aspirations; many more candidates for the Presidency come from the Senate than from the House.

Obviously, not every Senator is a candidate for the Presidency. But vanity leads many Senators, influenced by the prestige of their office and by their personal competition with the President, to allow personal bias to govern their votes on public measures. This is one of the reasons why personal animosity plays such a large role in the business of the upper chamber. One Senator, who is a philosopher as well as politician, recently told the author that long service in the Senate has led him to the conclusion that about one-third of the votes in this august chamber are dictated by animosity toward the President or toward fellow Senators. Of course, the merits of a measure, as well as the opinions of their constituents, and political expediency, have great weight with Senators. But, he insisted, notwithstanding all these factors, personal antipathy counts heavily. Having observed many foreign parliaments as well as American legislatures, he concludes that personal bias plays a larger part in the United States Senate than in the legislatures of Britain or Canada.

The history of the defeated treaties in the Senate is replete with the far-reaching effects of Senatorial animosity. The rancor of Henry Cabot Lodge toward President Wilson was chiefly responsible for the defeat of the Covenant of the League of Nations. The spite of Senator Charles Sumner for President Andrew Johnson was instrumental in rejecting the treaty of 1869 with Great Britain for the settlement of the *Alabama* claims. The bitter hatred of the Crawford Senators for John Quincy Adams, Secretary of State under

President Monroe, defeated the treaty of 1824 for the suppression of the slave trade.

Although similar animosities exist in the House, too, party discipline prevails more thoroughly in this larger legislative body, and the business of government is conducted in a more impersonal manner. Furthermore, the House is closer to the people than the Senate, so that the weight of public opinion, as reflected in the lower chamber, is not so liable to be blocked by a few individuals who act from personal pique or prejudice.

Eloquent testimony of the incapacity of the Senate to deal with minority obstruction is found in the filibuster. This trick for paralyzing the will of the majority was eliminated from the British House of Commons in 1881 and from the American House of Representatives in 1890. Unhappily, it is still used in the Senate, even in times of great national peril. In February, 1917, in the face of illegal German submarine attacks on American shipping, the House of Representatives passed the Armed Ship Bill by a vote of 403 to 14. The majority in the Senate was eager to concur. But a group of twelve Senators filibustered the bill to death. The country agreed with the sharp rebuke of the President, who said: "A little group of willful men representing no opinion but their own, have rendered the great Government of the United States helpless and contemptible."

At the next session of Congress, the Senate made an effort to amend its rules, but with little real effect. In the years since, not a single session of Congress has been free from these dilatory tactics, whereby a small minority frustrates the will of the majority. The one-man filibusters of Huey Long, the filibusters of southern Senators against antilynching bills, and filibusters and threats of filibusters by isolationist Senators when aid to the democracies attacked by Hitler was under consideration, have shocked and scandalized the nation.

In 1925, the House of Representatives, more responsive to public opinion than the Senate, voted for American adherence to the World Court. But the Senate, tortured with the personal ambitions of aspirants to the Presidency, and incapable of freeing itself from minority control, repeatedly blocked action. The House has been far ahead of the Senate in the struggle to free this country from the Neutrality Act of 1937, which impaired the defense of the democratic foes of the Axis powers, and assisted the aggressions of Hitler, Mussolini, and the Japanese militarists. Even so, the House lagged behind public opinion. As early as April, 1939, a Gallup Poll showed that 57 per cent of the American people were in favor of amending the Neutrality Act of 1937 in order to permit the sale of war materials to England and France in case of war in Europe, but not until November, more than two months after Hitler had declared war on Poland, was the act so modified.

In July, 1939, President Roosevelt, anticipating war, urged the repeal of the Neutrality Act. Leaders of the House of Representatives were responsive, but the obstruction of a few Senators, among them William E.

Borah, strangled the project. It was on this occasion that the President informed a White House conference of Congressional leaders that the dispatches of the Foreign Service indicated an outbreak of war in the near future. Borah replied that he had better sources of information than those of the Department of State, and that all of his informants assured him there would be no war. Six weeks later, Hitler declared war on Poland.

Recently, careful study of some of the Senators' records has brought startling evidence of the degree to which personal pique, animosity, and partisan bias influence Senatorial opposition to Presidential foreign policies. Such an analysis of Senator Burton K. Wheeler, of Montana, reveals that he can be expected to oppose almost any measure proposed by President Roosevelt. Senator Wheeler is a Democrat. So also is the President. Yet, the animosity of the senior Senator from Montana for the President is one of the well-known stories of Washington. Even its source is known. In 1933, the President failed to appoint Wheeler as Attorney General. The Senator had some claim to the office, and he has never forgiven the President for the oversight. A burning sense of fancied injustice has led the Senator to oppose measure after measure of the President.

If President Roosevelt, at the end of war, submits the peace settlement to the Senate, Senator Wheeler will probably oppose it. Irrespective of the treaty's merits, he will be apt to use every trick of obstruction to insure its defeat. Under the two-thirds rule of the Senate, and lacking the momentum of participation by the lower house, such tactics might succeed in rejection of the treaty. The Senator from Montana would also be likely to oppose any treaty negotiated by Wendell Willkie, if the titular leader of the Republican Party were President at the time of the peace settlement; for a "loyal" Democrat, like a "loyal" Republican, must oppose the treaties of a President of the opposite party. It is only the exceptional Senator who can rise above party loyalty, even in the field of foreign policy. Senator Wheeler is not the exceptional Senator.

Senator Robert A. Taft, of Ohio, is a competent lawyer and an estimable legislator. But his antipathy to Wendell Willkie is so devastating that it would be a miracle if he failed to oppose any kind of peace that Willkie as President might negotiate. Judged by past behavior and present attitudes, certain Senators can be counted upon to oppose any peace proposals made by certain Presidents.

So the count goes. In the obstructive minority one Senator is guided by personal animosity, another by partisan bias, and another by presidential aspirations. Of all the motives revealed by the analysis of the individual Senators, personal animosity seems to be as prevalent as partisanship.

Obviously, rancor, delusions of grandeur, and partisanship are stumbling blocks to the democratic process. The public interest is badly served and democracy languishes if the representatives of the people are guided chiefly by these motives. Fortunately, these are not the motives which prevail in either house of Congress. But subjecting the ratification process to the two-thirds rule in the upper chamber, where a few men, driven by rancor, ambition, and partisanship can thwart the will of the majority, constitutes a negation of the democratic process, and a danger to the peace of the United States.

There are historical reasons why the House of Representatives does not participate in the treaty-making process. Under the Articles of Confederation, the Congress was the sole organ of government; each State, great and small, had an equal vote, and a two-thirds majority was requisite for any decision. Every treaty was negotiated by ministers appointed specifically for this purpose by the Congress. In the Constitutional Convention of 1787, Alexander Hamilton, the strongest advocate of central government, proposed that the making of treaties be vested in the Chief Executive with the approval of the Senate. This view, which was considered a long step toward centralization of power, finally prevailed.

In one sense, the exclusion of the House of Representatives from treaty-making was part of the compromise between the large and small States which led to the "more perfect union" of all the States. The thirteen States, according to the argument of the small States, had won their independence as sovereign States by virtue of the Declaration of Independence of 1776, and the sovereignty of each State must be preserved. The Connecticut Compromise finally resolved the dispute between the small and the large States by the clever formula of adopting a bicameral in place of a unicameral legislature. To satisfy the large States, the people were to be represented in the House of Representatives in proportion to the population; to satisfy the small States, all States were to enjoy an equal voice in the Senate, namely, representation by two Senators from each State.

Closely allied to the States' rights doctrine was the theory that the President should be more or less the mere agent of the legislature. The Congress of the Confederation had possessed both executive and legislative powers, so that the small States were reluctant to consent to a division of powers, all the more so if the President were to be elected by the people rather than by Congress itself. Arising partly from the States' rights doctrine, came the theory that the Senate (representing the States), in addition to its legislative functions, should serve as an advisory council to the President. This led to the idea of delegating to the President, as agent of the Senate, some of the power to make appointments and conclude treaties. The upper chamber, in its capacity of executive council, would ratify treaties and confirm appointments.

Some of the members of the Philadelphia Convention objected to the exclusion of the people's representatives from a share in the ratification of treaties. James Wilson, an eminent jurist who, with Benjamin Franklin, represented Pennsylvania, proposed that treaties be approved by the entire legislature. Since treaties had the validity of law, he argued, they ought to have the same sanction as law. The argument that outweighed this cogent contention seems to have been merely the supposed necessity for secrecy. The President and twenty-six Senators could be trusted to keep a secret; but sixty-five Representatives could not! Said Roger Sherman: "The necessity of secrecy in the case of treaties forbade a reference of them to the whole legislature." Washington, Madison, and Hamilton, who had a good share of distrust of the common man, agreed with him.

The provision for the two-thirds rule was also a holdover from the days of the Congress of the Confederation. Under the Articles of Confederation, which Washington, Madison, and Hamilton had derided as detrimental to national prosperity and sound foreign policy, the ratification of treaties required the consent of two-thirds of the States. This relic of the weak Congress of 1777-1778 persisted in the plans discussed in the Philadelphia Convention. Again, it was James Wilson who eloquently argued that the two-thirds rule was undemocratic. Looking into the not-too-distant future, he warned his colleagues of the danger of minority control of foreign policy; but his excellent arguments were brushed aside by his compatriots. Some saw a need for a check on the Executive and others were devoted to the States' rights doctrine. The motion to strike out the two-thirds rule was lost.

The founders of the Republic wrote the doctrine of the separation of powers into the Constitution in unmistakable terms. The Constitution of 1787 entrusted the law-making function to the legislature; the law-enforcing function to the Executive; and the law-interpreting function to the judiciary. In their system of checks and balances, the Founding Fathers were not averse to an overlapping of functions, that is, that more than one organ of government might share in the performance of a particular task. It was not inconsistent to provide that both the executive and a part of the legislature should share in the treaty-making power. Treaty-making was considered to be legislation initiated by the executive; and a treaty was as much a law as a statute of Congress or the Constitution itself. This idea is expressed in Article VI (section 2) of the Constitution which reads:

> This Constitution, and the laws of the United States, which shall be made in pursuance thereof, and all treaties made, or which shall be made, under authority of the United States, shall be the supreme law of the land. . . .

The view that treaty-making is a legislative as well as an executive function has become generally accepted throughout the democratic world. Treaty-making in Great Britain was formerly considered solely as an executive power—a prerogative of the Crown. And even today, treaties, after negotiation, are ratified simply on the signature of the King. But under the British parliamentary system, the King is merely a figurehead, a symbol of government. Treaties are negotiated by the ministers, who exercise all the powers of the Crown in the name of the King. As the ministers are responsible to Parliament, which can dismiss them at any time by a vote of nonconfidence, it follows that the cabinet is extremely responsive to the legislative will.

Under the Parliament Act of 1911, Great Britain

enjoys a degree of democracy seldom found in other lands. By virtue of this statute, the House of Lords (the upper chamber) was shorn of its concurrent power over bills. Today, the Lords have no control over money bills and only a suspensive veto over nonfinancial bills. Literally, it is the House of Commons, representing the people of Britain, that alone rules the United Kingdom. Thus, in Great Britain, ministers who hold office only at the will of the majority of the House of Commons negotiate treaties which the King ratifies on the advice (better say, direction) of these same ministers. At the same time, the House of Commons has the opportunity to debate and approve or reject any treaty which the majority in the Commons may desire to consider.

In other countries which possess bicameral legislatures, both houses usually participate in treaty-making. In France, for example, a long list of important treaties could be ratified by the President of the Third Republic only after approval by both the Chamber of Deputies and the Senate. In Germany, under the Weimar Constitution of 1919, and until Hitler became *Reichskanzler* in 1933, the approval of the Reichstag was required for all treaties within the competence of the legislature. Argentina, Brazil, and most of the Latin American countries require ratification by a majority in both houses of the legislature. Only three Latin American states (Cuba, Mexico, and Ecuador) follow the example of the United States and give the upper chamber the sole power of consent to ratification.

The two-thirds rule and the exclusion of the House of Representatives from the treaty-making power were not the sole departure of the Constitution of 1787 from the path of democracy. The Connecticut Compromise giving one-half of the legislative power into the hands of an upper chamber representing States unequal in population was admittedly undemocratic. The Electoral College, providing for indirect election of the President was also not in keeping with the democratic process. Nor was the deliberate attempt to guard against the rise of political parties. The suffrage problem was settled in a manner far removed from Jefferson's definition of democracy; for only those who qualified as voters in each State had the federal suffrage. In New York, for example, voters for assemblymen had to own a freehold worth 20 pounds per year or pay rent of 40 shillings. Property and even religious qualifications prevailed in many States.

The framers of the Constitution did not regard their handiwork as perfect. Even Washington, Hamilton, and Madison doubted the ability of the new government to meet the needs of the young Republic. An amending process was provided in the Constitution itself, but its makers could not foresee how cumbersome their method of amendment would prove to be. When Washington, in his Farewell Address, reminded the American people that the Constitution could be amended, he was unaware of the extraordinary difficulties that would impede this procedure as the thirteen states increased to forty-eight.

In the century and a half of its existence, the Constitution has only seldom been amended by the method prescribed in it. Nevertheless, the Constitution has undergone a remarkable development, largely in a manner other than by the amending process. Judicial interpretations, statutes of Congress, amendment of State constitutions, and custom and usage have all had their share in the development of the Constitution. The Supreme Court has grown progressively more liberal in its interpretation of the Constitution, so that Congress today exercises powers which were never contemplated by the framers of the Constitution. Statutes of Congress, such as the acts regulating the operation of ships, railroads, telegraph and telephone, radio, and airlines, have expanded our federal constitutional law. Custom and usage have profoundly modified the fundamental law. The growth of political parties, and direct election of the President, have also come about by the slow force of custom, not by amendment.

Wishing to place the election of the President beyond the reach of the people and to prevent the rise of political parties, the framers of the Constitution devised the Electoral College. This was to consist of wise statesmen selected in a manner determined by the legislature in each State. These Electors were to meet every four years, and after careful deliberation, they were to select the best qualified man in the country to serve as Chief Executive. The Electoral College was also intended as a safeguard against the appearance of political parties, which both Washington and Hamilton regarded as a positive menace to good government. The Electoral College still remains, but only as a legal fiction. Today, our President is elected directly by the people, and despite the ban upon political parties, these are now accepted as one of the most useful elements of government.

This evolution of American constitutional law has steadily pressed in the direction of greater democracy. Amendments, too, have done their share. The Civil War Amendments (XIII-XV) freed the slaves and guaranteed their civil and electoral rights. The Seventeenth Amendment, in 1913, put the election of Senators in the hands of the people of the States, in place of the indirect or oligarchic procedure determined by each State legislature. The Nineteenth Amendment, in 1919, granted women the right to vote.

Though much of the Constitution has been liberalized beyond anything that the framers dreamed of, the provision for ratification of treaties has retained its original undemocratic mold. Suffrage has been broadened, slavery abolished, direct election of the President established, political parties permitted to exist, and the rights and interests of the common man more completely protected. But in foreign policy, this country still retains its archaic, oligarchic, and anti-social procedure of ratification of treaties.

The negotiation of treaties in the United States conforms to canons of democracy. It is the President of the United States who negotiates; the Secretary of State and ministers plenipotentiary, who actually carry on the negotiations, are his subordinates. This practice conforms with constitutional law in most modern countries. Almost universally, the negotiation of treaties is considered to be an executive function; the consent to ratification of treaties, a legislative function.

Under the Constitution, the negotiation of treaties follows a democratic procedure, for the President, who is responsible for the negotiation of all treaties, is elected by the whole people of this country. Indeed, the President and the Vice-President are the only federal officers who represent all the people in the United States. When the President, personally, or through his Secretary of State, negotiates an agreement with foreign representatives, he is acting in behalf of all the American people. Secrecy may be necessary at various stages of the negotiations, but there is nothing undemocratic in that kind of concealment. The covenants, when finally signed by all the negotiators, are open to the inspection of all citizens.

The exclusion of the Senate from the process of negotiation is not a violation of democracy. By its nature, the negotiation of treaties is an executive process. The exchange of views and the bargaining required in the reaching of an international agreement is a process in which a national legislature cannot readily participate. In almost every modern government, therefore, the executive negotiates the treaty and then lays the completed document before the legislature for approval.

The words "advise and consent," as found in the treaty-making clause of the Constitution, seem to imply that the President should consult the Senate at every step of the negotiation of a treaty. This is not, however, the practice. The sharp separation be-

tween the negotiation and approval of treaties tradi-
tionally followed in the United States grew out of a
curious episode in the administration of George Washington on the occasion of the negotiation of one of
the earliest of the treaties of the new republic.

On August 21, 1789, President Washington informed the Senate that on the following day he would
meet the upper chamber to advise with the Senators
in regard to the negotiation of a treaty with the Chero-
kee Indians. The Senate was a little nonplussed by the
announcement and there was some worry as to the
proper manner in which to receive the President. This
question, however, was resolved upon the President's
arrival by giving him the Vice-President's chair. The
President handed John Adams, the Vice-President,
seven articles of a proposed treaty to be read to the
Senate. He evidently expected the Senate to debate,
amend, accept or reject the articles, while he answered
questions and explained the views of the Executive.

The Senate, however, was uncomfortable in the
presence of the great man. The Senators were reluctant
to debate in the hearing of the Chief Executive. After
considerable fumbling, Robert Morris moved that the
question of the treaty be referred to a committee. The
motion carried. This was a polite method of informing the President that his presence was not desired.
Washington, however, was a little slow to take the hint.
He arose and angrily said: "This defeats every purpose
of my coming here." At last the President grasped the
fact that the Senate desired his departure. As William
Maclay recorded in his diary: "A pause for some time

ensued. We waited for him to withdraw. He did so with a discontented air. Had it been any other man than the man whom I wish to regard as the first character in the world I would have said with sullen dignity." William H. Crawford, in relating the incident many years later, said that after his cold reception by the Senate, Washington declared that "he would be damned if he ever went there again."

Naturally, the rigid separation of the negotiation of treaties from their approval has led to many clashes between the Senate and the Executive. We have already seen how Adams' treaty for the suppression of the slave trade, Tyler's treaty for the annexation of Texas, Hay's arbitration treaties, and Wilson's peace settlement were rejected in bitter contests between the Senate and the President.

Woodrow Wilson, while a professor of politics at Princeton University, advised Presidents to avoid these clashes by consulting with individual Senators during treaty negotiations. What man does not like to be consulted? What man does not resent the ignoring of his opinion in matters that concern him? Senators are no exception to the general rule. Unfortunately, Woodrow Wilson, as President, did not follow his own advice. His neglect to coax, wheedle, or take counsel with Henry Cabot Lodge was partly responsible for the defeat of the Covenant of the League of Nations in 1919.

However, even in the matter of consultation, Senators are hard to satisfy and will criticize the President, whatever method he pursues. In 1898, President Mc-

Kinley desired to terminate the Spanish-American War with a treaty acceptable to the Senate. Accordingly, he appointed three members of the Senate Committee on Foreign Relations on the commission of five to negotiate the treaty of peace. His action, however, was sharply denounced in the Senate as a violation of the Constitution and an infringement upon the prerogatives of the upper chamber. He was warned to refrain from attempts to win support for a treaty in advance of its submission to the Senate by the appointment of Senators as negotiators.

One by one the oligarchic features of our Constitution have been replaced by democratic institutions. The progress in democracy has been accomplished by amendments to the Constitution, judicial interpretation, and custom and usage. The ratification of treaties, however, is one of the remaining aspects of our Constitution which belong to the eighteenth rather than the twentieth century. It is nothing less than a perpetuation of minority rule and a negation of the democratic process.

CHAPTER FOUR

THE LEAGUE-OF-NATIONS FIASCO

THE League of Nations was one of the most controversial questions in the history of American public opinion. Even today it remains a subject of dispute. Some hold that the American desertion of the League of Nations in 1919 destroyed all chance of the Versailles system to preserve world peace and thereby contributed to the conditions that led to World War II. Others still consider the League to have been an instrument of British and French policy, from which America was wise to withdraw. Still others are convinced that the League was only a weak universal peace system, and that a strong military alliance of democratic powers was the prime requisite for the preservation of the peace. According to these last, the mistake of 1919 was the dissolution of the alliance of the victor states and the substitution of a universal league that appeared to frown on defensive alliances.

I have no intention of discussing these differing viewpoints here. The only phase of the question which concerns us now is the fact that the Treaty of Versailles, with reservations proposed in the Senate, commanded a simple majority in the upper chamber, and was defeated only by lack of a two-thirds majority. The method by which a minority in the Senate forced rejection of the Treaty is not without importance in the history of the conduct of American foreign relations.

In the Armistice of November 11, 1918, both victors and vanquished accepted the Fourteen Points proposed by President Woodrow Wilson as the basis for peace. The fourteenth of the Fourteen Points called for the creation of an association of nations for the purpose of affording mutual guarantees of political independence and territorial integrity to great and small states alike. This was to be the means for "keeping the world safe for democracy." At the Paris Peace Conference, President Wilson doggedly insisted that the creation of a League of Nations, to serve as an agency of permanent peace, could not be postponed to some indefinite future date, and that the Covenant of the League should be included in the peace treaties themselves. He won his point against opposition in the British, French, Italian, and Japanese delegations. The Covenant of the League became the first part of the Treaty of Versailles, and later of the Treaty of St. Germain (with Austria), of the Treaty of Trianon (with Hungary), and of the Treaty of Neuilly (with Bulgaria).

European acceptance of Wilson's peace plan was one of the greatest triumphs in American diplomacy. As the Peace Conference drew to a close, the negotiators at Paris grew more tolerant of this American scheme, influenced, no doubt, by general public approval. Indeed, before the Conference adjourned the utility of the League as a means of determining many questions that could not be settled at the Paris Conference became apparent, so that the doubts of the negotiators were finally resolved into actual enthusiasm for this new instrument of government.

In July, 1919, the President brought a copy of the Treaty of Versailles to Washington, confident that it had the support of the American people, and that it would be promptly approved by the American Senate. All the devices for gauging popular opinion at that time indicated wide support for American membership in the proposed League. Comment in the newspapers, not only on the Atlantic seaboard but also in the Middle West, was more favorable than unfavorable. Senator James E. Watson, of Indiana, who received from Senator Henry Cabot Lodge a secret appointment to manage the opposition to the Treaty in the United States Senate, said to Lodge: "Senator, I do not see how we are ever going to defeat this proposition. It appears to me that eighty per cent of the people are for it. Fully that percentage of the preachers are right now advocating it, churches are very largely favoring it, all the people who have been burdened and oppressed by this awful tragedy of war and who imagine that this opens a way to world peace are for it."

A small minority was able to defeat the Covenant of the League of Nations in the Senate. Paradoxically, most of the Senators in this minority belonged to the same party as the men who originated the idea of the League. The project of the League of Nations was first broached by leaders of the Republican Party when, in the winter of 1914-1915, a group which included former President William Howard Taft, George Wickersham (Attorney General under President Taft),

A. Lawrence Lowell (President of Harvard University), Theodore Marburg (minister to Belgium under President Taft), and Hamilton Holt (editor of the *Independent*), organized the League to Enforce Peace. Hamilton Holt was the only man in the group who was not a Republican. Later, their project received the blessing of a most distinguished Republican, Elihu Root.

Unfortunately, after winning the support of the President, the League to Enforce Peace failed in its educational campaign to win the support of Congress and the American people. Some speaking tours were made and former President Taft made a number of notable addresses; but there was no systematic propaganda program such as the one which the William Allen White Committee conducted in behalf of aiding the Allies in 1940 and 1941.

President Wilson submitted the Treaty of Versailles to the Senate on July 9, 1919. On March 19, 1920, it was returned to the President without the Senate's consent to ratification. The Paris Peace Conference had spent some five months in drafting the Treaty; the United States Senate spent eight months in defeating it. The result of these months of confused conflict was clear. Under the two-thirds rule, the Senate was able to refuse approval of the Treaty, and without this approval the Treaty could not become American law. A study of the motions on the various reservations to the Treaty as well as on the Treaty together with the reservations shows that while only twenty-one Senators favored the Treaty without reservations, a majority approved the Treaty with reservations. For instance, on March 19, 1920, the resolution to approve the Treaty with fifteen reservations received 49 affirmative votes as against 35 negative votes. That was a majority of the 96 votes in the Senate, but not a two-thirds majority. If these ballots had been cast under a constitutional provision requiring only a majority of Senators present for ratification the Treaty with reservations would have become American law.

President Wilson's selection of two of the five members of the peace delegation was none too fortunate. The delegation consisted of himself as head, Robert Lansing (the Secretary of State), Colonel Edward M. House (personal adviser to the President), General Tasker Bliss (military adviser), and Henry White (a Republican career diplomat). Instead of the last two, it would have been a masterstroke to have selected former President Taft and Elihu Root. It is probable that the Covenant of the League would have been much the same, even had Taft and Root assisted as negotiators, although Taft ardently desired an international police force which was not included in Wilson's League. But had Taft and Root gone to Paris, the "irreconcilable" Republicans in the Senate would have found it difficult to reject a treaty which had been negotiated and signed by such notable leaders of their own party.

Finally, the President's insistence that the Treaty of Versailles be ratified without drastic amendment or reservation blocked compromises in the Senate which might otherwise have permitted ratification. Much can be said for this uncompromising attitude of the President. The Treaty had been negotiated at Paris under great difficulties. It was the result of many delicate compromises among the negotiators. The foreign offices of America's allies assumed that the Treaty would be ratified by all the signatory powers without amendments or reservations. In a loyal effort to keep faith with the other signatory powers, the President demanded that the Senate, like the British House of Commons, vote approval of the Treaty without alterations.

When the President became fully aware of the strength of the Senate opposition, he attempted to carry an appeal to the American people, over the heads of Senators. Leaving Washington on September 3, he began a nationwide speaking tour. Traveling as far west as California and Oregon, he made thirty-nine notable speeches. But, after delivering a powerful address at Denver, he succumbed to great physical and mental fatigue. Returning to Washington, the President suffered a paralytic stroke. Thereafter, an almost helpless invalid, confined to the White House, the Chief Executive was in no mental condition to reach an understanding with leaders in the Senate who might have saved the Treaty from the wrath of its opponents.

The defeat of the Treaty of Versailles in the Senate was largely the achievement of one man, Henry Cabot Lodge, senior Senator from Massachusetts. Paradoxical indeed was Lodge's opposition to the League of Nations. In 1906, as a member of the Committee on

Foreign Relations in the Senate, he had favored American participation in the Conference of Algeciras, and at that time he had even proposed that America should underwrite the peace in Europe. After the outbreak of World War I, Lodge was among the first to demand a rupture with Germany. In 1916, he supported Taft's plan for a League to Enforce Peace.

But bitter jealousy of President Wilson, coupled with fancied slights, caused Lodge to attack the President on every occasion. In December, 1918, the Massachusetts Senator publicly warned the Allies that the Senate had the power to reject any treaties that did not please it. In March, 1919, after the tentative draft of the text of the League Covenant had been made public, he inserted in the *Congressional Record* a round robin signed by thirty-seven Republican Senators condemning this draft, and even proposing that the negotiation of the Covenant be postponed until the peace with Germany had been signed.

This action was in keeping with an earlier intrigue against the President. Lodge gave Henry White, before he sailed for Paris, a memorandum on the Senate's views regarding the peace settlement. This he asked White to show, in strictest confidence, to leading Allied statesmen in the hope of strengthening their hands against the program of President Wilson. Only the most impelling of personal antipathies could have driven an otherwise honorable man like Senator Lodge to commit such an act of treachery.

The defeat of the Treaty of Versailles is almost entirely due to the astute parliamentary tactics of

Senator Lodge. The Republicans had won the Congressional election in November, 1918, so that when the Sixty-fourth Congress convened in May, 1919, the Grand Old Party, for the first time in six years, had command of the Senate. The majority of one, however, was obtained only by the seating of Truman H. Newberry as Senator from Michigan, although he was then under indictment and later convicted of violation of the Federal Corrupt Practices Act and sentenced to two years in prison. As chairman of the Republican Conference (party caucus) in the Senate, Lodge controlled the appointment of the Committee on Committees. He took the chairmanship of the Committee on Foreign Relations for himself and proceeded to pack this Committee with opponents of the Treaty of Versailles, in order to insure from the start an unfavorable report on the Treaty. This fact is known through several witnesses, one being Senator Frank B. Kellogg, of Minnesota, to whom Lodge promised a place on the Committee if he would agree to oppose the Treaty.

While Lodge could easily control a packed Committee, it was not certain that he could force the defeat of the Treaty on the floor of the Senate. Too many Republican as well as Democratic Senators were in favor of the principle of a league of nations. And so, with consummate cunning, he decided to destroy the Treaty by indirection. Explaining to Senator James E. Watson, of Indiana, whom he had appointed his secret assistant in organizing the opposition to the Treaty, he said: "I do not propose to try to beat it by direct frontal attack, but by the indirect method of reservations." To Allen T. Burns, he confided that he expected to defeat the Treaty in the same manner that the Senate had vetoed the Taft arbitration treaties in 1911, namely, by reservations of such drastic nature as to destroy the effectiveness of the agreements.

Accordingly, Lodge left the leadership of the irreconcilables, Republicans who advocated outright defeat of the Treaty, to Senator William E. Borah (Idaho) and Hiram Johnson (California), while he openly assumed leadership of those Senators who welcomed reservations. The fourteen Lodge reservations were designed to emasculate the peace system; even if the Treaty had been approved with all the weakening reservations, Lodge confidently counted on a final defeat of the Treaty because of the President's stubborn refusal to ask the Allied Powers to accept such reservations.

Of the irreconcilables (Senators opposed to the Treaty either with or without reservations), twelve were Republicans and three were Democrats. On the other side of the Senate, twenty-one Democrats stubbornly followed the President in demanding unconditional approval of the Treaty. Between these two camps were about fifty Senators, both Republican and Democrat, who either insisted upon reservations or else were willing to accept reservations as a compromise. By playing the middle against both ends, Lodge was able to win his astonishing victory. The fourteen Lodge reservations, badly as they cut away the Treaty, were adopted by votes averaging about 50 ayes to 40 nays. The resolution to consent to ratify the Treaty

without reservations was rejected by a vote of 38 to
53—a severe defeat for the supporters of the President. .
The final resolution on March 19, 1920, on consent to
ratification with reservations received 49 yeas and 35
nays. The resolution lacked seven votes of a two-thirds
majority. It was a triumph that amazed even Lodge
himself.

Professor Denna Frank Fleming's admirable studies
and those of other scholars have shown that in reality
more than two-thirds of the Senators were in favor of
American membership in the League of Nations. But
Senator Lodge manipulated the Senators' differences
so skilfully that every compromise rendered the defeat of the Treaty under the two-thirds rule all the
more certain.

Senator Porter J. McCumber (North Dakota), the
only Republican Senator who voted for the Treaty
without reservations, complained that the Senate debate was conducted not on the merits of the Treaty but
on wholly irrelevant matters. The opponents of the
League, he charged, gave little heed to the laudable
purpose of the Covenant, and they offered no other
adequate alternative for world peace.

The Senator was correct. A flock of specious arguments filled the lengthy tirades against the Covenant.
It was claimed that American participation in the
League would result in surrender of American sovereignty, involvement in foreign wars, the reversal of
our traditional policy and the Monroe Doctrine, a
destruction of American principles of democracy, the
submission of domestic questions to international de-

termination, and the annihilation of international good faith. Seldom in the history of Congress has debate sunk to such a low level of misrepresentation and sophistry. Lindsay Rogers, in *The American Senate,* characterizes the contest in these words: "It is literally true that the strength of convictions of the speakers was directly proportioned to the ignorance and tyrociny of Senators in foreign politics. Too many Senators made addresses based on the knowledge of a mediocre college undergraduate, increased by resort to a couple of war books and the *Encyclopedia Britannica,* and presented with the argumentative skill of the average lawyer." *

The arguments against the League, pusillanimous as most of them were, did not conceal the real motives of opposition to the Covenant. Although sincere doubts as to the wisdom of American participation in the League doubtless motivated some Senators, the majority of the opponents of the League were guided by three other incentives: (1) partisanship; (2) personal bias and emotional reaction toward the President; and (3) senatorial jealousy of its constitutional prerogatives.

It is one of the regrettable aspects of American politics that the leaders of a political party will seek to destroy a President's foreign policy and jeopardize the peace of the world, not because the policy is in itself bad, but rather because these leaders are determined to discredit the President and destroy his political in-

* From *The American Senate,* by Lindsay Rogers, published by F. S. Crofts & Co., New York, N. Y.

fluence. Such was the case in 1919. Political antago-
nisms had existed even during the war, in spite of the
supposed adjournment of politics. The President's
ill-advised demand for the return of a Democratic
Congress, prior to the Congressional election of November, 1918, did not help to assuage the bitter opposition to his leadership. However, the President's
address to voters would hardly seem sufficient justification for a deliberate plot of Republican leaders to
smash the peace policy of the Paris Conference, in
order to win the presidential election of 1920.

Letters exchanged between Henry Cabot Lodge and
Albert J. Beveridge show that Beveridge, Lodge, and
George Harvey (editor of *Harvey's Weekly*) coolly
selected the Covenant of the League as the issue on
which to defeat the Democratic Party in the election
of 1920. Beveridge was convinced that if President
Wilson won the consent of the Senate to ratification of
the Treaty of Versailles, the prestige of the President
would become so great as to sweep the Democratic
Party into office in the forthcoming presidential election. In other words, unless the President was defeated
on the Treaty issue, the Republican Party would face
another four lean years.

Like Lodge, former Senator Beveridge had been at
one time a supporter of American participation in
international co-operation. His speeches on foreign
policy both in and out of the Senate breathed the spirit
of a strong foreign policy and the abandonment of
isolation. That such a distinguished scholar and politician as Beveridge so completely reversed his position

on external relations indicates the intensity of the party spirit that dominated the group of Republican leaders who were largely responsible for the defeat of the treaty.

Another reason for the defeat of the Covenant was the personal animosity of several Democrats and Republicans to President Wilson. The Covenant was viewed as his achievement. Ratification of this agreement would add to his well-earned laurels and ensure his great international prestige. His personal enemies in the Senate, therefore, were determined to destroy this prestige if it were in their power to do so.

We have already mentioned Henry Cabot Lodge's bias, a bias almost amounting to a disease. An educated, scholarly, and refined statesman, he hated the President with an intensity that warped his intellect. It was almost pathologic—a brilliant man obsessed with the passion to destroy the prestige of a fellow creature because of a fancied slight to his undoubted competence.

Theodore Roosevelt also played some part in stirring up opposition to the international policies of the President, although such opposition was inconsistent with Roosevelt's previous record as an internationalist. As early as 1910, in a memorable address at Christiania, Roosevelt had called upon the Great Powers to form "a League of Peace, not only to keep peace among themselves, but to prevent, by force if necessary, its being broken by others." His almost violent opposition to the President's proposal of a League of Nations can therefore be attributed only to his hatred of a man whom he loathed and despised, whom he considered partly responsible for his defeat in the presidential election of 1912 and partly responsible for blocking his appointment to the command of a division of troops on the battlefield of France. Unhappily, Roosevelt cultivated, as his biographer Pringle put it, "the gospel of vengeance."

The Senate numbered many lesser personages whose views on the Treaty of Versailles were partly influenced by their animosity toward the schoolmaster in the White House. Among these Wilson-haters were Frank B. Brandegee (Connecticut), Albert B. Fall (New Mexico), Hiram W. Johnson (California), Philander C. Knox (Pennsylvania), George H. Moses (New Hampshire) and James A. Reed (Missouri). In some respects these Senators reflected the detestation of, if not malice against, Wilson that was found in all parts of the country. Senator Thomas Walsh (Montana), in a mild rebuke to some of his colleagues, said with truth: "Nine out of ten letters I get in protest against this Treaty breathe a spirit of intense hatred of Woodrow Wilson, and I am led to believe that this feeling forms a large element in the opposition to this Treaty; but I am astonished that Senators should allow considerations of this character to influence their judgment."

The magnificent role played by William Howard Taft somewhat restores our faith in human nature. Though he had every reason to detest Wilson as the candidate who had defeated him in the three-cornered presidential election of 1912, Taft, when he became convinced that world peace could be accomplished only by the creation of a league of law-abiding states, undertook to persuade Wilson to share this view, with the success which we have already described. Ignored by the President in the selection of the American delegation to the Peace Conference, Taft nevertheless loyally supported the Covenant as drafted in Paris, although he was disappointed in the character of the proposed League of Nations. He desired a "league with teeth in it," in other words, an international police force. But, being a realist, he was glad to accept a compromise.

After the publication of the text of the Covenant, Taft defended this draft in eloquent addresses in New York, Philadelphia, and other cities. When the Treaty was laid before the Senate, he came to Washington in the humble capacity of lobbyist for the Wilson Covenant. He was astonished by the intensity of the hatred of Wilson which he found in the Senate. A record of a conference with Senator Frank B. Kellogg reads as follows: "He found Senator Kellogg in a state of great nervousness, convinced of impending defeat. Kellogg broke out into damning of the President and of the Treaty. He said he wished the Treaty was in Hell. When asked whether he was for the Treaty, he said he was. Taft asked him, therefore, whether it was not his duty as a Senator to fight for what he believed was right, rather than to give way to feelings of hatred toward Wilson and to mere nervous weariness of the whole subject? Kellogg made Taft very impatient, and he lost his temper. He said that Kellogg had no guts to stand up and make the fight."

Appalled by the almost unnatural obsession of some Senators for revenge against the President, Taft sought to appeal to public opinion in a new series of eloquent addresses. In one of these notable speeches, addressed to industrial leaders, he said: "There is a depth of misconception in respect to the situation that makes one marvel at the ignorance of you businessmen. You accept statements from Senators stung with hatred of Wilson, as the businessmen of the country are, and who imagine that Wilson is merely postponing reconstruction to gratify his fad. That is not true in any degree. I don't like Wilson any better than you do, but I think I can rise above my personal attitude in order to help along the world and the country. I don't care who gets the credit for the League of Nations if it goes through."

A third motive of opposition to the Covenant was senatorial jealousy of its constitutional prerogatives. One of the phenomena which objective observers of government find disturbing is the narrow view which officeholders often take of the importance of their particular constitutional position. Without a broad view of the functions of governmental agencies, or of the most efficient means of serving the public welfare, such public servants frequently demand the continuance of their authority on the sole ground that the Constitution has given them such jurisdiction. Perhaps, it is suggested to them, the Fathers of the Republic made a mistake, perhaps the times have changed and the old provisions of the Constitution are out-moded, perhaps the Constitution requires amendment. "No," says the officeholder, "the Constitution has given me this authority and it must not be abated!" The prestige and vested interest of a few officeholders are thus placed above the welfare of the people.

A large part of the debate on the Treaty of Versailles was devoted to the argument that the Covenant constituted an encroachment upon the constitutional powers of the Senate. In the first place, it was argued, the President had violated the Constitution in not consulting the Senate previous to the negotiation of the Treaty. This argument, advanced by Lodge, Knox, Cummings, Kellogg, and others, was unrealistic. Consultation with the Senate in the negotiation of treaties is contrary to American tradition. Ever since the day in 1789 when President Washington was rebuffed by the Senate, it had been the custom of the President to negotiate treaties without consulting the Senate and to lay the treaty before the Senate for ratification after the negotiations had been completed. As a young scholar, Senator Lodge had taught history in Harvard College, but in the Senate debate on the Covenant his memory for history proved exceptionally weak.

Rebuked for their historical inaccuracy by supporters of the President, the League opponents branded the Covenant as an attempt at executive usurpation of power. They claimed that, in violation of the Constitution, the Covenant exalted the Chief Executive to the position of dictator. It permitted him to usurp the authority of Congress to declare war; it granted him perpetual war powers; and it conferred on him the right to ignore the Senate in making international agreements. The irreconcilables claimed that the Constitution provided that the Senate should be the advisory council of the President in the negotiation of treaties; but, they said, the Covenant destroyed the treaty-making powers of the Senate and reduced this august body to a secondary role in foreign affairs. None of these charges was true.

The defeat of the Covenant of the League of Nations in the United States Senate is one of the most spectacular episodes in the diplomatic history of this country. Henry Cabot Lodge fulfilled his boast. He mutilated the Treaty with such devastating reservations that the supporters of the Administration could not accept the mutilated convention. Even so, a majority of the Senate supported the Treaty with reservations. On the final test the Treaty lacked only seven votes of a two-thirds majority. Under the two-thirds rule, a minority of bitter partisans and personal enemies of the President were able to sabotage the peace system which America had persuaded Europe and Asia to accept.

CHAPTER FIVE

WILL EXECUTIVE AGREEMENTS BY-PASS THE SENATE?

AMERICAN political genius is adept in leaping over constitutional barriers. Devices for circumventing the Constitution have sometimes rested heavily on the consciences of hard-pressed Presidents. But at least these statesmen have had the satisfaction of knowing that their decisions protected the public interest or promoted the national welfare, a satisfaction that must have been all the greater when they recalled the difficulties of overcoming constitutional obstacles.

It is not the purpose of this book to discuss the political ethics of avoiding the Constitution by indirection, but merely to confine attention to the practical needs of the United States, and the effect of its acts upon its allies in the United Nations.

The United States is approaching the end of a great and costly war. This Government has taken steps to participate in the organization of a United Nations for the purpose of maintaining the peace in a postwar world. These steps have received the emphatic approval of the American people. Under such circumstances, shall the President place the peace settlement in the usual form, namely a treaty of peace, and allow it to be mutilated, if not totally destroyed, by a minority in the Senate? Or, shall he seek devices for insuring American participation in the organization for peace? These are the practical questions which have to be faced by a practical Chief Executive.

In the summer of 1943, members of Congress became aware of two facts. First, Secretary of State Cordell Hull, the principal agent of President Roosevelt in foreign affairs, planned to participate in the creation of the agencies of the United Nations one by one, instead of establishing the complete peace system in one great international act. Second, the pacts creating the agencies of the United Nations would be in the form of executive agreements rather than treaties. Congressmen were slow to grasp the significance of this momentous decision. Some thought it was merely a bluff in order to win a commitment from both houses of Congress. Only a few realized that the Secretary of State was in dead earnest.

The United Nations had gotten off to a good start on the basis of an executive agreement. The Declaration of the United Nations, signed at the White House on January 1, 1942, was nothing else than such an agreement. Although it was not a treaty, no doubts had been cast on its binding effect on the twenty-six states which signed it at that time, or on the seven other states that subsequently adhered to the Declaration. The President had negotiated this alliance by virtue of his constitutional powers as Commander-in-Chief of the Army and Navy and as spokesman for the American people in foreign affairs.

The Mutual Aid Agreements with Great Britain, Soviet Russia, China, and twenty other allies in the war against Nazi aggression also were executive agreements, but of a different kind. These had been authorized by the Lend-Lease Act of 1941. In like manner, the trade agreements designed to lower tariff barriers had been authorized by the Trade Agreements Acts of 1934, 1937, and 1940. But the Declaration of the United Nations rested on no such Congressional delegation of authority.

Could the Department of State go further in the organization of the United Nations without authorization from Congress? The astute Secretary of State thought it could. In May, 1943, the United States took the leading role in a United Nations Conference on Food and Agriculture, at Hot Springs, Virginia. In conformity with the Final Act of this Conference, which was an executive agreement and not a treaty, the Washington Government participated in a new United Nations Interim Commission on Food and Agriculture. Finally, on June 10, the Department of State announced that it had negotiated a "draft agreement" for a United Nations Relief and Rehabilitation Administration with Britain, Soviet Russia, and China. This agreement was to be laid before the other twenty-eight members of the United Nations and the eleven "associated nations" for their adoption.

The Relief and Rehabilitation Administration Agreement was clearly intended to set the pattern for many other postwar agencies. The distribution of aid to the peoples in the areas liberated from the Axis yoke was to be placed under control of a Central Committee responsible to a Council of the United Nations.

As a possible guide for future pacts, the "draft agreement" was far more important than it appeared at first glance.

Alarmed at the far-reaching consequences of a series of postwar pacts without the consent of Congress, the Connally Sub-committee of the Senate Committee on Foreign Relations sought the conferences with the Secretary of State which have been mentioned in a previous chapter. In these conferences, Senators Connally, Thomas and Green spoke for the Democrats. Senator Arthur H. Vandenberg assumed the task of representing the Republicans. Between them they sought to develop an understanding with the Secretary that would permit the participation of Congress in the negotiation of post-war pacts. In turn, the State Department would receive the authority of the national legislature for negotiating such agreements.

The compromise eventually developed by Senator Green and Assistant Secretary Sayre relied upon the use of the joint resolution. Adoption of a resolution of this character would require only a majority vote in the two houses of Congress. This arrangement would by-pass the minority obstruction in the Senate, while permitting both houses to have a hand in pact-making. Obviously, the postwar agreements that would result from this understanding between Congress and the State Department would still have the status of executive agreements and would not be treaties. The formula, however, seemed fair to both Congress and the President. At the most, it was an easy solution of a stubborn problem. Some critics thought it might prove too easy.

The proposed Connally-Vandenberg or Green-Sayre formula for participation of Congress in the negotiation of postwar pacts has led politicians and jurists to reappraise American conduct of foreign affairs. Irreconcilable isolationists see in the formula the blasting of their hope to lead a retreat from the international scene at the termination of hostilities. Supporters of American participation in the postwar peace system are confronted by the pertinent question: Can executive agreements adequately take the place of treaties in the creation of the new society of cooperating states? The problem merits most serious study, for it might prove disastrous for the future peace to have the United Nations built on a faulty legal basis.

An executive agreement, like a treaty, is a contract or compact between two or more states. Hunter Miller, in the preface to his collection of *Treaties and Other International Acts of the United States,* accepts the connotation that a treaty, in American law, is an international act submitted for the advice and consent of the United States Senate. All other international compacts of the United States are executive agreements.

American archives are replete with executive agreements. The first use of this type of agreement under the Constitution appears to have been as early as 1792, when Timothy Pickering, the Postmaster General under President Washington, negotiated arrangements for the exchange of mail between the United States and other countries. He acted by authority of the Post Office and Post Roads Act, passed by Congress in the same year. Since then, executive agreements have been used not only in promoting the postal service but also in trade agreements, tariff regulation, aviation and radio control, acquisition of territory, lease of naval bases, arbitration claims, membership in international unions, and even in the termination of treaties. Recently, we have had the spectacular Hull-Lothian Agreement of September 2, 1940, whereby the United States acquired a ninety-nine-year lease on naval bases from Newfoundland to British Guiana in return for fifty destroyers delivered to Britain.

About nine hundred treaties have been proclaimed by Presidents of the United States from the inauguration of the Federal Republic in 1789 to the opening of World War II in 1939. Over two hundred other treaties were concluded which never became law because they were rejected by the Senate, or neglected by the Senate, or amended in a manner not acceptable to the other signatory powers. In the same period, over twelve hundred agreements with foreign countries were entered into and enforced without securing the advice and consent of the Senate to these contracts. All of these other compacts were executive agreements. They were made and enforced by the Executive without reference to the Senate.

The use of the executive agreement thus exceeds that of the treaty by nearly 40 per cent. The bulk of executive agreements have been of somewhat routine nature, while the greater number of the momentous pacts of the United States have been in the form of treaties. The majority of the executive agreements are two-party contracts, while most of the great multipartite compacts (contracts between three or more signatory powers) are in treaty form. There are exceptions: the compacts under which the United States has entered the Universal Postal Union, the Pan American Union, and the International Labor Office, as well as the United Nations have been multipartite executive agreements.

The authority of the President to make many kinds of executive agreements is unquestioned, nor is there any doubt as to the power of Congress to authorize him to do so. The former power comes from the President's constitutional authority as an organ of foreign relations and as Commander-in-Chief to enter into agreements with foreign governments. The power of Congress to authorize the President to enter into agreements is easily implied from the so-called "eighteen powers" of the First Article of the Constitution. Numerous decisions of the Supreme Court have supported the validity of agreements which are within the President's authority. Many executive agreements of this character do not bind only the administration entering into them; they are part of the law of the land, and must be observed by succeeding Presidents.

An executive agreement may become a treaty from one day to the next. For instance, the understanding between Great Britain and the United States for determining the naval armament on the Great Lakes, made in the form of an executive agreement, was negotiated in 1817 by Charles Bagot (Minister of Great Britain) and Richard Rush (Acting U. S. Secretary of State). It was put into immediate effect. A year later, as an after-thought, President Monroe submitted the agreement to the Senate, which promptly consented to its ratifi-cation. Another executive agreement which became a treaty was the agreement of 1905 with the Dominican Republic. To forestall German intervention, Presi-dent Theodore Roosevelt directed the negotiation of an agreement which guaranteed the territorial integ-rity of the Republic and placed the customs revenues in the hands of the United States. When the agreement was submitted to the Senate as a treaty, the Adminis-tration failed to muster the necessary two-thirds vote for ratification. Thereupon, the President put the agreement into effect without the approval of the Senate. He was bitterly criticized by the Senate, and was called some harsh names. The President refused to bow to the upper chamber; and two years later the Senate approved the treaty. This, however, made no change in the operation of the agreement, which had been in effect for two years.

The procedure in negotiating treaties and execu-tive agreements is the same. The two kinds of agree-ments may also be much the same in form. The Decla-ration of the United Nations, signed by twenty-six states at war with Nazi Germany at the White House on January 1, 1942, is in the form of a treaty, without, of course, the usual provision for the ratification of the compact. On the other hand, the celebrated Open Door Agreement regarding China, which Hay negoti-ated in 1900 with Britain, Russia, Germany, France,

Italy, and Japan was in the form of an exchange of diplomatic notes. It was specified at the time that these notes had the same effect as a treaty.

If executive agreements have the same effect as treaties, why not use them always as substitutes? If the making of executive agreements conforms to the democratic process, while our system of making treaties violates the principles of democracy, why not choose executive agreements rather than treaties? Dr. Wallace McClure in his *International Executive Agreements: Democratic Procedure under the Constitution of the United States* asks these questions. His argument, in brief, is as follows:

(1) The two-thirds rule governing the Senate's approval of treaties is not only undemocratic but also has produced stalemates in time of crisis which are a peril to national welfare. (2) The same legal effect can be accomplished by an executive agreement as by a treaty; they are interchangeable methods. (3) For more than one hundred and fifty years, executive agreements have been employed in the United States as an alternative to treaties. They are a part of our constitutional law and American tradition, and are fully sanctioned by the Supreme Court. (4) Employment of executive agreements is in no way a violation of the Constitution even if they largely replace treaties. The President was intended to have, under the Constitution, all the powers and functions of the head of a state in the family of nations. He has authority to enter into any manner of international act with other heads of states on any subject that is not in contraven-

tion of the Constitution or in conflict with an act of Congress. (5) The President can do by executive agreement anything that he can do by treaty, provided Congress by law co-operates, and there is also a wide field of action in which the co-operation of Congress is not necessary. *Therefore,* it is feasible, constitutional, and desirable to substitute executive agreements extensively for treaties. Under this procedure, the will of the majority would not be frustrated by a willful minority. In the future, no international act need be defeated by the two-thirds rule in the Senate.

No one defending the Senate's prerogative has satisfactorily answered Dr. McClure. The only way to meet the charge that the two-thirds rule and the Senate's monopoly of consent to ratification is undemocratic is to place the approval of treaties, by a constitutional amendment, in the hands of a simple majority of the members of both houses of Congress. But the champions of vested interests and of minority controls do not wish this to happen. They set the prerogatives of the upper chamber above the will of the majority.

When the principle of the separation of powers was written into the Constitution, it was never intended to forbid complete co-operation between the President and Congress. After all, both organs of government exist for the welfare of the American people and not as ends in themselves, and a little teamwork between the two offices is all to the good.

In the interest of co-operative government, the executive agreement has much to offer, and in certain fields of international action its use is greatly to be preferred to that of treaties. One of these fields is international economic co-operation, and especially tariff agreements. The tariff on foreign goods entering this country has been one of the most controversial questions in our political history. Members of Congress, regardless of party, are apt to take a sectional rather than a national view on this issue. The fate of the twelve treaties negotiated in 1899 and 1900 by John Hay well illustrate this. Under the two-thirds rule there was no hope of their approval by the Senate. Indeed, under this rule there is practically no chance for the approval of any treaty which makes economic concessions, even on a strictly *quid pro quo* basis.

The Trade Agreements Act of 1934 which was renewed in 1937, 1940, and 1943 created a sounder technique for the negotiation of agreements for reciprocal reductions of the tariff. The Act gave the President the power to enter into agreements with foreign countries for the decrease or increase of existing tariff rates by 50 per cent. Under it, Secretary of State Cordell Hull has negotiated twenty-seven reciprocal agreements. It is believed that these agreements did much to revive foreign trade, after the tragic slump during the economic depression of 1929 to 1933. And even more is expected from the operation of the Hull agreements in the postwar world.

On the occasion of the enactment of the Trade Agreements Act in 1934 and on its three subsequent renewals, it faced bitter attacks from vested interests as well as from the opposition party. Obviously, the President, in asking Congress to authorize him to enter into these agreements, had in reality requested the legislature to pass a self-denying ordinance. A trade agreement with Germany lowering the import duties on farm machinery might please the farmers but certainly would displease the manufacturers. A trade agreement with Canada lowering the American tariff on wheat and the Canadian tariff on automobiles would gratify the manufacturers but would certainly meet the opposition of the farmers in the United States. Logrolling is a favorite legislative trick. In the case of the German and Canadian agreements, the representatives of the farmers and of the manufacturing interests would unite to defeat both agreements. They have acted in this manner in the past; they may be expected to act in the same manner in the future. Under the two-thirds rule, all trade agreements are doomed in the Senate. Even under the system of the joint resolution, requiring only a majority of members present in each house of Congress, many trade agreements would be rejected.

The conflicts of interest that will hamper the revival of an enlightened trade policy in the postwar world were displayed in the contest over the renewal of the Trade Agreements Act in the year 1943. The addresses of Vice-President Wallace, Secretary Hull, and Undersecretary Welles stressed the need for co-operative planning on a world-wide scale, in order to remove the economic barriers which indirectly contribute to war. These arguments meant little to the Republican opposition.

Under the presidential form of government, in

which the opposition party has no responsibility for the conduct of government, it is difficult for opposition leaders to refrain from opposing everything that the party in power proposes. Thus, Charles L. McNary, of Oregon, leader of the Republican minority in the Senate, demanded that Congress retain the right to veto any trade agreement within sixty days after negotiation. This proposal, had it been carried, would have vitiated the entire system. As damaging was the amendment proposed by Senator Danaher (Connecticut), which would terminate all the twenty-seven agreements six months after the war either by a joint resolution of Congress or by a presidential proclamation. The acme of futility was contained in an amendment offered by Senator Francis Maloney (Connecticut and a Democrat) which would require all future trade agreements to be ratified, like treaties, by a two-thirds vote of the Senate.

The opponents of reciprocal tariff agreements find the Trade Agreements Act a flagrant evasion of the Constitution. The friends of the Hull Agreements think that the act is in keeping with the legitimate development of the power to govern, and that it is highly conducive to the welfare of this nation. To date, no one has been able to convince the federal courts that he has suffered an injury by the operation of the act.

The Trade Agreements Act must be taken into consideration in discussing any modification of the treaty-making power in the United States. The field of international economic co-operation, and especially the lowering of tariff barriers, requires exceptional procedure. Even if the Constitution were amended so as to abolish the two-thirds rule and give the House of Representatives a share in treaty-making, the exigencies of the modern world would still require a procedure for making trade agreements different from that for other treaties. So far as American constitutional law is concerned, the Hull formula adequately meets the needs of the twentieth century in the matter of trade agreements.

Advocates of the executive agreement make much of the cumbersome process of amending the Constitution. At the time the Constitution was written, they say, no one foresaw how difficult the amending process would become in a country as extensive and full of conflicting interests as the United States in the twentieth century. It is extremely hard to obtain the two-thirds vote in both houses of Congress, indispensable for a joint resolution submitting a proposed amendment to the States. The proposed amendment must then be ratified by the legislatures or conventions of three-fourths of the States. The alternative method of calling a new Constitutional Convention at the request of two-thirds of the States has never been used.

Proponents of the substitution of executive agreements for treaties as a means of avoiding the minority veto power in the Senate are able to point to many well-known precedents for changes without constitutional amendment. The technique they propose is consistent with the development of American constitutional law. It is in line with a rational reconciliation of our rigid Constitution with the continuous growth and change in national life, a reconciliation that has been consistently followed for more than a century.

There are, however, very real objections to the substitution of executive agreements for formal treaties. Executive agreements are made between the heads of states and, when followed by legislative resolutions or statutes, have all the effect of law within the countries concerned. But it is questionable whether they have the same prestige or sanctity as the duly ratified treaty.

Some doubt exists as to the continuing obligation of executive agreements on succeeding Presidents. For instance, an exchange of notes, such as the Lansing-Ishii Agreement of 1917 on Japanese "special interests" in China, has been deemed morally and politically binding upon the administration that negotiated it, but not upon its successor. Some executive agreements, therefore, cannot be considered as a part of the law of the land.

For many years law-abiding states in the family of nations have urged the necessity for preserving the pledged word. President Roosevelt, Prime Minister Churchill, Secretary Hull, and other statesmen of the democracies have reiterated the declaration that the present war is being waged to vindicate the sanctity of treaties. The rule of *Pacta sunt servanda* (pacts must be obeyed) has become the very foundation of the society of nations.

The binding effect of international contracts does not depend entirely upon the validity of the process by which they are made. They must also be written in the hearts of the people. If they are founded on public approval, the heads of states may be less likely to violate their terms whenever they expect to secure a national advantage therefrom. This means that the negotiation and approval of the treaty must strike the popular imagination as an act that solemnly places the entire nation under a sacred obligation.

In the past, treaties have served as the vehicle of this solemn engagement of public faith. They constitute the proof of agreement among the negotiators. When reinforced by the ratification of the respective legislatures, they become endowed with the solemn sanction of all of the representatives of the peoples of the signatory states. Nothing can be more binding upon the national conscience in all states.

Executive agreements, unfortunately, are not endowed with this symbolic significance. Although the heads of states cannot easily be dissociated from their governments, an agreement reached between executives, even when supported by joint resolutions of the legislatures, lacks, in the popular mind, that impression of solidarity of mutually accepted obligations, which comes from the solemn covenant negotiated by the Chief Executive and approved by the legislature in the very same form as signed by the ministers plenipotentiary.

Without question, executive agreements are preferable to treaties as the vehicle of certain kinds of international acts, such as agreements regarding economic co-operation, tariffs, postal service, regulation of radio and air navigation, and leasing of naval bases. But a more solemn procedure is advisable for the great multipartite agreements which furnish the constitutional basis of the organization of the family of nations and of codes of international law.

The agreements growing out of World War II will become the legal foundation of the new peace system. The Atlantic Charter of 1941 and the Declaration of the United Nations of 1942 lead one to believe that in the future all states will make solemn commitments for the maintenance of international peace. It is hoped that these commitments will be made in very definite terms, and will be most scrupulously observed. Both the Atlantic Charter and the Declaration of the United Nations in their present form are merely executive agreements. It is true that the Atlantic Charter is viewed as the announcement of the peace aims of the United States and Great Britain as well as their allies in the contest against the Axis Powers. It is also true that the Declaration of the United Nations is a pledge of the heads of the states of the United States, Great Britain, Soviet Russia, China and twenty-eight other countries that after the defeat of Nazi Germany they will co-operate in establishing a new peace order founded on the principles of the Atlantic Charter. But both of these agreements are no more than pledges for the adoption of later agreements which will be constitutional or fundamental in nature.

Agreements for the establishment of the Combined Chiefs of Staffs (the United States and Great Britain), the Combined Food Board, the Combined Raw Materials Board, and the Inter-American Defense Board may well be in the form of executive agreements. Obviously, the mutual-aid agreements under the Lend-Lease Act belong in the same category. Executive agreements conveniently provide for the Relief and Rehabilitation Administration, and for AMG (Allied Military Government), and may do so for a commission to try international criminals, for the lease of naval and air bases, and for the initial arrangements for an international police force. Indeed, the governing council of the United Nations may, in the first instance, be set up by such an agreement. The permanent Council is foreshadowed in the proposed Council of the United Nations for supervision of the Relief and Rehabilitation Administration as provided in the "draft agreement" described earlier in this chapter. But the definitive constitution of the United Nations, the revival of the World Court, and the mutual guarantees of the Four Freedoms (freedom of speech and religion, freedom from want and fear) definitely require the solemn engagement of formal treaties.

Although executive agreements may in all cases, and must in some cases, have the approval of both houses of Congress, there is no uniform practice as to the submission of the agreements to the legislature. The Atlantic Charter and the Declaration of the United Nations have never been submitted for Congressional approval, and may never be submitted. The continuance of this practice, however, will not make for stability in international commitments. The President, indeed, represents the American people. But the people have other agents in Washington—representatives who come from the Congressional districts and the States. Solidarity of agreement requires that all national representatives be drawn into the orbit of the national commitments.

The association of both the executive and legislative representatives in the negotiation and acceptance of international commitments will fortify the validity of these agreements. Indeed such procedure may well be the *sine qua non* of their endurance. Furthermore, the democratic process demands the association of the legislative branch with the executive. In the great struggle with the Axis Powers, the democracies have been confronted with states in which the legislature has been completely subservient to the executive. The *Führer* principle, like military supremacy in Japan, means the suppression of the constitutional legislature. Devotion to democratic principles as understood in America and Britain requires the intimate partnership of both branches of government in the acceptance of international commitments.

The British parliamentary system (where the executive is dependent on the legislature) lends itself more readily to the co-operation of the organs of government than does our presidential method which has merits of a different character. Under the separation of powers adopted by the Fathers of the Constitution, both the Chief Executive and the national legislature labor under an enormous handicap in the matter of concerted action. But, the very prominence of the principle of separation of powers as embodied in our Constitution should make our Chief Executive doubly anxious to allow the legislature to participate in international commitments. The day always comes when commitments must be fulfilled. The fulfillment of most of the commitments growing out of World War II will require the co-operation of the national legislature. Hence, the need for joining Congress in all promises of this character.

Although American constitutional law has had a remarkable growth through custom and usage, the continuous practice of openly avoiding the fundamental law is dangerous. Such tactics may be tolerated or may even be advisable in times of national crisis. The annexation of Texas by joint resolution in 1844, and of Hawaii in 1898, although evasions of the Constitution, are justifiable on the ground of public necessity. And, in like manner, many other evasions of the supreme law may be condoned. But the constant evasion of the Constitution cannot do otherwise than to breed a contempt for law that is dangerous for democratic institutions.

The use of executive agreements as a substitute for a peace settlement is a palpable evasion of the fundamental law. The Constitution is clear and unambiguous on the subject of treaties. An international act of the United States can be a treaty only if it receives the advice and consent of two-thirds of the Senators present. It is possible that if the Supreme Court should be asked to pass on the validity of an agreement which posed as a treaty, the court would be compelled to find the agreement void because it had been adopted by means that were not in accord with the Constitution.

The pronouncement that a treaty already in effect was null and void in the United States because it had been made in an unconstitutional manner might create a major international crisis. It would destroy the confidence of our allies in our integrity, and would endanger the whole peace system.

Under international practice and convenience, a peace settlement which serves as a new constitutional basis for the family of nations has always taken the form of a solemnly ratified treaty. This does not imply that the fundamental law of international society cannot rest on other foundations than treaties. Custom and usage contribute heavily to the law of nations. But a permanent peace settlement, as we have already seen, requires specific commitments from the member states of the peace system. Such commitments require the form of national pledges of the most solemn nature. Lacking this form, the commitments mutually given and received will not inspire the highest degree of confidence which in turn will bring the maximum of international co-operation.

An international agreement which is obviously an avoidance of the Constitution of the United States will not inspire the maximum of confidence from our allies in the United Nations. It may give weight to the lurking suspicion that the form of the commitment might serve as a ready excuse for repudiation of the obligation. The proposed Green-Sayre formula calling for the use of joint resolutions may be useful in the creation of some of the agencies of the United Nations. It will be tolerable as the means for sidestepping the constitutional process, if a selfish minority in the Senate should block an amendment to the Constitution for the reform of the ratification of treaties. But it is inadequate for placing the final peace settlement on a sound and permanent basis.

CHAPTER SIX

WE ARE IN THE UNITED NATIONS NOW

THE new American peace policy requires implementation. American opinion, on the whole, does not go so far as to favor the creation of a superstate or of a Federal Union. We are not disposed to surrender our sovereignty; nor are we willing that the national state cede even part of its exclusive control over all persons and property within its boundaries. What we desire is the execution of a policy of international co-operation which will take place within the states system or the family of independent nations.

Small states, like the Scandinavian countries, may find it to their advantage, to accept Winston Churchill's advice to federate. As members of a federation within the family of nations, they may have a voice in the Council of the United Nations more in keeping with their resources. But the people of the large states will surely desire to retain the states system and to try the experiment of maintaining peace by a plan of loyal co-operation within this system.

The United Nations, then, are expected to operate as a universal agency of member states, each of which will retain its independence and sovereignty. To make this policy effective, the member states within the United Nations will perhaps have to adjust their organs of government, in order to secure the maximum of co-operation within the states system. Constitutional reform of this character involves no loss of independence and no derogation of sovereignty. It is merely an attempt to insure more readily, by means of faithful co-operation by every member state, the achievement of the policy for which the United Nations were created.

This is the task. What are the means for its fulfillment, so far as the United States is concerned? Is the American system of government adequate for the role which the people of the United States desire to play in the peace system? Can our federal government meet the diplomatic problems of the twentieth century? If the United States is to take a leading position within the United Nations, its organs of government must be adjusted to the new function of international collaboration in such a manner as to secure the greatest degree of achievement.

A survey of our constitutional system shows that the President holds adequate authority to participate effectively as our Chief Executive in international government. Congress, also, has sufficient power, organization, and procedure to perform its functions as a legislative body within the new peace system. The one exception is the ratification of treaties and the possibility of minority control in the Senate. Though the co-operation between the Executive and the Legislature is not so smooth as that in the parliamentary form of government, yet, as in the past, we must depend upon the moderation of President and Congress in the interest of the public welfare. The modernization of our constitutional system requires: (1) the democratization of our treaty-making process; and (2) the promotion of full co-operation between the President and Congress.

Faults are readily seen in others, but not so readily in oneself. We excoriate the constitutional defects in Nazi Germany and militaristic Japan; and quite rightly so. The political defects in Germany, Italy, and Japan, and even in some of our Allies, since they make for war, will have to be corrected, if peace is to prevail within the states system. Americans, however, hesitate to admit that our faulty ratification process may be a menace to world peace as surely as is the *Führer* principle in Nazi Germany, or dual diplomacy in Nippon. But this defect should be confessed in all candor, and corrected. If we insist on constitutional reforms in our defeated foes, we can afford with magnanimity to put our own house in order. Unless we do so, our co-operation with our colleagues in victory will always be in jeopardy.

Collaboration within the United Nations will require: (1) Acceptance of binding commitments regarding consultation, employment of armed forces, guarantees against aggression, and economic co-operation. (2) Acceptance of minor and temporary commitments from time to time as political and economic conditions change. (3) Constant consultation with member states in order to secure peaceful change of the *status quo* in the interest of justice and peace. (4) Development of codes of international law which shall govern the relations of states within the states system.

Effective collaboration under (1) will require political alliances within the system of collective security. Undoubtedly, one of the weak features of the League of Nations was the Wilsonian doctrine of discouraging alliances within the universal peace system. The new United Nations should serve as the vehicle for a global system of security. This should not preclude alliance of the Big Four (the United States, Britain, Soviet Russia, and China), which will have the responsibility for maintaining the monopoly of weapons, as envisioned in the Atlantic Charter. At least in the beginning, the international police force will needs be in the control of the great powers which have borne the brunt in the destruction of Nazi aggression. The Big Four can direct the international police only through an alliance, which, of course, will have to be of military character.

The American people expect their government to assume its fair share in the giving and receiving of commitments required for the development of the new peace system. But how can our government perform this function adequately if compelled to rely upon a treaty-making process in which a small minority can destroy the whole policy of commitments? The new Green-Sayre formula for authorization of postwar pacts by a joint resolution of both houses of Congress will facilitate the creation of many agencies of the United Nations. But it does not adequately solve the problem of the constitutional basis of the new peace system. If the experiment of making peace secure through the United Nations fails, we shall be on the road to the Third World War. It is not too much to say that the peace of the world as well as of the United States rests in some measure on the abolition (or evasion, if abolition is impossible) of the undemocratic power of the American Senate to veto treaties.

Public opinion is an extremely important factor in the conduct of foreign relations in our day, so that whatever information can be gathered is of more than passing interest. Do the American people desire the United States to participate as a member state in the United Nations? Are they ready to make the sacrifices required for effective leadership in the maintenance of a peace system? The answer is emphatically in the affirmative.

In July, 1942, a Gallup Poll showed 59 per cent of the people to be in favor of American participation in some form of a league of nations after the war. Exactly 22 per cent opposed the proposition and 19 per cent were undecided. As the war progressed, popular sentiment moved more and more toward international cooperation. In December, 1942, another Gallup Poll posed the question: "Should the government take steps now, before the end of the war, to set up with our Allies a world organization to maintain the peace of the world?" The replies showed 73 per cent of the people on the affirmative side and only 27 per cent on the negative. Of the voters who had cast a Democratic ballot for President in 1940, there were 75 per cent in favor of immediate planning and only 25 per cent opposed. Of the Republican voters, 69 per cent favored planning and 31 per cent opposed it. Finally, in June,

1943, came the Gallup Poll described in Chapter One, which showed 78 per cent of the people in favor of active American participation in the postwar peace system. Only 13 per cent registered an unfavorable answer, and only 9 per cent were undecided.

A Gallup Poll, published on May 1, 1943, and covering forty-eight States, showed 74 per cent of the American people in favor of an international police force as proposed in the Ball-Hill-Burton-Hatch Resolution. Only 14 per cent were opposed and 12 per cent had no opinion. Another Gallup Poll, limited to persons who could give an argument for or against an international police force, published on September 27, 1943, showed 75 per cent for such a force, 17 per cent against it, and 8 per cent with no opinion.

Public opinion polls also show that a majority of the American people support close ties with Great Britain. A Gallup Poll, published on September 8, 1943, gave 61 per cent of American citizens to be in favor of a permanent American-British postwar military alliance, 25 per cent opposed, and 14 per cent undecided. A nation-wide survey by the National Opinion Research Center (University of Denver), released on September 18, 1943, showed that 70 per cent of the American people approved United States membership in a world union. Four per cent gave qualified approval; 13 per cent opposed; and 13 per cent were undecided.

The American people had gone far on the road of internationalism when the voters of Milwaukee, in the Congressional election of 1942, chose a Representative like Professor Howard J. McMurray, who frankly advocated the plan of Federal Union proposed by Clarence Streit. Or, when Hennepin County in Minnesota elected such an ardent interventionist as Dr. Walter H. Judd. In the same election, however, the people of Illinois returned to the Senate the mouthpiece of the Roosevelt-baiting *Chicago Tribune* as well as a Congressman-at-large who was proved to have had traffic with Nazi agents.

In the summer of 1943, some twenty Congressmen made bipartisan tours through the States on behalf of the Ball-Hatch Resolution. This resolution, introduced in the Senate on March 16, 1943, called upon the President to summon conferences of representatives of the United Nations for the purpose of creating a permanent international organization. The public response to the addresses delivered in several hundred cities and towns was more than favorable. It indicated a wide appreciation of the need for the new American peace policy and the determination to give it political support even at great personal sacrifice.

Resolutions of legislatures in thirteen States show the same trend of public opinion. In 1942, the legislature of Montana passed a joint memorial to the President and Congress advocating international order and world peace by policing power with full co-operation and responsibility of the United States. This memorial was adopted partly as a rebuke to the arch isolationist, Burton K. Wheeler, who represents the State in the Senate. The legislatures of Vermont, Pennsylvania, and Massachusetts have passed resolutions in support of

American participation in international co-operation. On March 26, 1943, the Assembly and Senate of New York voted a resolution urging the President and Congress to promote an international organization of all nations to maintain a lasting peace. In May, 1943, the legislature of Alabama adopted a memorial in support of the Ball-Hatch Resolution.

The legislatures of four States—North Carolina, Maryland, Rhode Island, and Alabama—have passed very advanced resolutions, drafted by a North Carolina lawyer, Robert Lee Humber, declaring that "all peoples of the earth should now be united in a commonwealth of nations to be known as the Federation of the World." In 1942, the Florida legislature, at the prompting of Clarence Streit's Federal Union, unanimously adopted a memorial requesting the President and Congress "to call at the earliest possible moment a convention of representatives of all free peoples to frame a federal constitution under which they may unite in a democratic world government subject to ratification by each people concerned."

Three other States—New Jersey, New Hampshire, and Connecticut—have passed resolutions calling for study of the problem of world federation. All of these resolutions are far in advance of public opinion, even in the States concerned. World federation is one of the most radical plans for universal peace. The fact that seven State legislatures have adopted measures indicating some inclination in this direction shows how far American opinion has advanced out of the era of isolation.

Many American citizens have been led to support international co-operation through the eloquent words of Roosevelt, Churchill, Wallace, and Hull. Others have been impressed by the vivid phrases of Wendell Willkie, the titular leader of the Republican opposition. But most Americans have reached this conclusion by observation of the hard, cold facts of international life in an age of totalitarian warfare. They have taken account of the retreat of the United States from the peace system of 1919 and have been shocked at its calamitous consequences. They have seen the menace of Nazi dictatorship and Japanese militarism to American peace and the peace of the whole world. These facts have been more eloquent than learned treatises on the interdependence of nations.

One of the amazing phenomena of our national politics is the lag between public opinion and the response to it in the Senate. Judging by public opinion polls based on the most scientific methods, the American people in the summer of 1939 were strongly in favor of modifying the Neutrality Act. Yet the leaders of the Senate refused to act. We have already mentioned the Gallup Poll of May, 1943, which showed 74 per cent of the American people in favor of an international police force, 14 per cent as opposed, and only 12 per cent as undecided. On the same date, an Associated Press canvass of the Senate recorded 24 Senators in favor of an international police force, 32 Senators as opposed, and 40 Senators who declined to commit themselves. Disregarding the Senators who were too evasive or too timid to state their views, this survey indicates that the majority of Senators are still out of step with public opinion in the field of foreign policy.

How can this discrepancy be explained? Perhaps it cannot be unriddled in any way that would be flattering to the Senate. At any rate, the average age of the American voter is thirty-six. The average age in the Senate is sixty-one. The minds of some of the Senators are frozen; they are not receptive to new ideas, nor can they set aside their deep-seated prejudices in the interest of the public welfare. Furthermore, some of the Senators are completely out of touch with their own constituents. In the last years of his incumbency, Senator Borah, for example, could hardly be said to have represented the real opinions of the people of Idaho. Today, Senator Hiram Johnson is little more than a California myth. In 1941, not a few Senators ignored honestly conducted polls in their states which showed that their bitter opposition to many American defensive measures against Hitler did not express the opinion of their own constituents.

All of this does not sufficiently explain the Senate's lack of response to public opinion. It accounts for only a small minority of the Senate—perhaps the same minority that would be found in almost any representative body. For lack of a better explanation, the following hypothesis is advanced.

An incomplete survey of the House of Representatives in the summer of 1943 indicated that the lower chamber was more favorable to American participation in the new peace system as proposed by President Roosevelt than was the Senate. This suggests that the

House is more willing to examine the foreign policy of the Administration on its merits, and does not tend to oppose it simply for the sake of opposition. The assumption by the Senate that it is an executive council designed to check the Chief Executive in foreign policy helps to arouse suspicion and opposition on the part of Senators toward almost every move of the President. This tendency plays into the hands of those Senators who are guided by personal prejudice, animosity, and love of prerogative, as well as of those who are active or latent candidates for the presidency.

The opportunity for unlimited criticism also gives individual Senators a chance to build reputations that otherwise would not be possible. In the Senate as elsewhere, some men are great in their own right, while some men can achieve a nation-wide reputation only by their attacks on great men.

Burton K. Wheeler, for instance, is a competent lawyer who can prosecute or defend a criminal case with a more than average ability. But he has a destructive rather than a constructive mind, and has won a wide reputation almost entirely because of his incessant attacks upon a great man. He is given a good press because newspapermen know that he is always ready with a caustic tirade against the President. He has put himself at the disposal of associations which oppose the President's foreign policy, and by hundreds of public addresses has built a notable reputation by his vindictive attitude.

The conclusion is obvious. The outmoded theory of the Senate as an executive council, authorized to approve or veto the acts of the President, invites the obstruction of men who fancy themselves to be the rivals of the Chief Executive. The abolition of the Senate monopoly on consent to ratification, therefore, might eliminate one of the motivating reasons for opposition to the President's foreign policy on other grounds than its merits. There will always remain the temptation on the part of the party out of power to oppose the President for the mere sake of opposition. But, at least, one evil—the opportunity for a minority of ambitious Senators to destroy a foreign policy through an undemocratic procedure—will have been eliminated.

In view of the dangers of minority rule, and of the present undemocratic character of the Senate, the President would be morally negligent if he submitted the Peace Treaty of the Second World War to the upper chamber without first securing a personal pledge from two-thirds of the Senators that they would vote for this agreement. Under the Constitution, the President has a solemn responsibility to the American people for the conduct of foreign affairs. His duty does not end with the negotiation of a treaty which he submits to the Senate with the hope that the upper chamber will prove equally faithful in the performance of its duty. On the contrary, he has the obligation—moral as well as legal—to take every constitutional precaution to avoid rejection of a treaty by an obstreperous minority in the Senate. The peace and welfare of his fellow citizens whom he represents are at stake. Obviously, international collaboration cannot be maintained if treaties negotiated in good faith by heads of states are ruthlessly rejected by a minority group in one of the signatory states.

It is not pleasant to contemplate the fate of the Peace Treaty at the end of World War II, should the President carelessly submit it to the Senate without the proper assurances. As usual, the Treaty would be referred to the Senate Committee on Foreign Relations. The present chairman is the picturesque Tom Connally, of Texas. There are fifteen Democratic members and eight Republican and Progressive members. The membership of the Committee, in order of seniority, is as follows:

SENATE COMMITTEE ON FOREIGN RELATIONS

Majority

Tom Connally, of Texas
Walter F. George, of Georgia
Robert F. Wagner, of New York
Elbert D. Thomas, of Utah
Frederick Van Nuys, of Indiana
James E. Murray, of Montana
Claude Pepper, of Florida
Theodore F. Green, of Rhode Island
Alben W. Barkley, of Kentucky
Robert R. Reynolds, of North Carolina
Joseph F. Guffey, of Pennsylvania
Guy M. Gillette, of Iowa
Bennett Champ Clark, of Missouri
Carter Glass, of Virginia
James M. Tunnell, of Delaware

Minority

Hiram W. Johnson, of California
Arthur Capper, of Kansas
Robert M. La Follette, Jr., of Wisconsin
Arthur H. Vandenberg, of Michigan
Wallace H. White, Jr., of Maine
Henrik Shipstead, of Minnesota
Gerald P. Nye, of North Dakota
James J. Davis, of Pennsylvania

Some of the most stalwart defenders of international co-operation in the Senate are members of the Committee, among them being Connally, Thomas, Wagner, Pepper, Barkley, and Glass. It also contains some of the most outspoken opponents of American participation in a co-operative peace system, including Clark (Missouri), Reynolds, Johnson (California), La Follette, Shipstead, and Nye.

Let us suppose that the Peace Treaty, negotiated by a Democratic President and submitted to the Senate during the Seventy-eighth Congress, provided for an international organization of the United Nations as proposed by the Ball-Hatch Resolution. It may be assumed that the majority of the Democrats on the Committee on Foreign Relations, through party loyalty, would support the Treaty. Senators Clark (Missouri), Reynolds, and Van Nuys could be counted upon to desert the party. The Republicans, with the exception of Senators Vandenberg, White, and La Follette, would probably vote unanimously against the Treaty. The vote in the Committee would then show something like thirteen to ten in favor of the Treaty. This is an uncomfortably narrow margin. If even one of the Democrats and the one pro-treaty Republican should waver, the Treaty could not even escape from the Committee without an adverse report. Even so, the Treaty would be in a more fortunate position than was the Covenant of the League of Nations in 1919, for on that occasion, the Committee on Foreign Relations had been thoroughly packed by Senator Lodge with opponents of the Covenant.

However, this does not mean that the majority on the Committee would force a prompt and favorable report on the Treaty, for the minority would demand public hearings, in order to inaugurate its strategy of delay and calumny. The majority would acquiesce because objection to this procedure might be interpreted as attempted concealment of damaging facts, and also because pertinent information might be obtained by questioning officials of the Department of State.

Thus, precious time would be consumed in protracted hearings, in the same manner that the opponents of the Lend-Lease Bill, in January through March, 1941, fiddled while Rome burned. The Secretary of State and other officials would be summoned. Every effort would be made by the minority to trap them into the admission of unfavorable evidence. Questions would be posed, as they were by Johnson, Nye, Clark, Reynolds, and La Follette in the Lend-Lease hearings, simply to give vent to spleen, prejudice, rivalry, and contempt for the President. Isolationists would be summoned from all corners of the country to continue the process of delay. Even Colonel Lindbergh might be called from retirement to criticize the conduct of the war in the air. He was the star witness of the obstructionists in the Lend-Lease hearings, and he may still be useful. Just as Gerald L. K. Smith, William J. Grace, and other doubtful witnesses were used as time-wasters by the isolationists in the hearings of 1941, it is not unlikely that similar witnesses would be recruited for the hearings on the Treaty. Probably a large pacifist representation would be brought before the Committee.

The hearings would terminate before the complete exhaustion of public patience. The Democratic majority of the Committee on Foreign Relations would then proceed to the adoption of a favorable report, provided one Democrat and Senator Vandenberg had not changed their minds. Otherwise, the new Republican-Democratic majority would write an unfavorable report. Eventually, both a majority and a minority report would be laid before the Senate. The former would probably advise ratification without amendments. The latter would probably offer amendments of such character as to destroy the integrity of the Treaty and to fill our allies with dismay.

The leadership of the opposition to the Treaty on the floor of the Senate would lack the generalship of Henry Cabot Lodge, who so skilfully marshaled the forces of obstruction against the Covenant of the League of Nations. There is no one among the Senate irreconcilables today who possesses the knowledge of foreign affairs and urbanity of Lodge. Leadership of the fight against the Peace Treaty would be either in the hands of Burton K. Wheeler, of Montana, who was floor leader of the opposition to the Lend-Lease Bill in 1941, or else in the hands of an informal committee composed probably of Wheeler, Nye, Clark, and Hiram Johnson, and possibly Vandenberg.

The debate on the Committee report would un-

doubtedly be public. The minority would insist upon
wide publicity, hoping by an appeal to antiforeign
prejudice and the moral backwash of the war to win
some popular support. The debate would be as bitter
as, but perhaps more informed than, was the debate on
the Treaty of Versailles. It would be as partisan as the
debates on the amendment of the Neutrality Act in
1939, or the passage of the Lend-Lease Act two years
later. It is not unlikely that the foes of the Treaty
would resort to the filibuster. This dilatory device was
used by Senator Wheeler in the Lend-Lease debate.
If he should be commanding the forces in opposition
to the Treaty, the filibuster would probably again be
brought into service.

The opponents of the Treaty, should it be voted on
in the Seventy-eighth Congress, might number as
many as forty-four members of the Senate. On the
basis of their past records and recent utterances, the
opposition would probably include the following
Senators:

PREDICTION OF SENATORIAL OPPOSITION TO THE PEACE TREATY

Democrats (18)

Chavez (New Mexico)
Clark (Missouri)
Clark (Idaho)
Johnson (Colorado)
McCarran (Nevada)
McKellar (Tennessee)
Maloney (Connecticut)
Murdock (Utah)
O'Daniel (Texas)

Overton (Louisiana)
Radcliffe (Maryland)
Reynolds (North Carolina)
Smith (South Carolina)
Tydings (Maryland)
Van Nuys (Indiana)
Wallgren (Washington)
Walsh (Massachusetts)
Wheeler (Montana)

Republicans (26)

Aiken (Vermont)
Brewster (Maine)
Brooks (Illinois)
Bushfield (South Dakota)
Butler (Nebraska)
Capper (Kansas)
Danaher (Connecticut)
Gurney (South Dakota)
Hawkes (New Jersey)
Holman (Oregon)
Johnson (California)
Langer (North Dakota)
McNary (Oregon)

Moore (Oklahoma)
Nye (North Dakota)
Reed (Kansas)
Revercomb (West Virginia)
Robertson (Wyoming)
Shipstead (Minnesota)
Taft (Ohio)
Wherry (Nebraska)
Tobey (New Hampshire)
Vandenberg (Michigan)
Wiley (Wisconsin)
Willis (Indiana)
Wilson (Iowa)

Progressive (1)

La Follette (Wisconsin)

Included in the list of irreconcilables are the thirty-two Senators who were recorded in the Associated Press survey of April, 1943, as opposed to an international police. To this number are added those Senators whose record indicates that they would be likely to vote against the peace treaty. Senator Robert A. Taft who since the Associated Press survey was made has joined Professor James T. Shotwell in support of an international police force, is nevertheless included in the list. It is believed that the party allegiance of the Ohio Senator is so strong that he would vote against any treaty negotiated by a Democratic President, and for almost any treaty negotiated by a Republican President.

Some clues as to the probable opposition to the peace treaty can be found in the debates in May and June, 1943, on the renewal of the Trade Agreements

Act. The final vote on the act in the Senate was 59 to 23, or more than a two-thirds majority. But the votes on the Danaher, O'Mahoney, and Maloney amendments failed to show a two-thirds majority in support of democratic control and international co-operation. The amendment offered by Senator John A. Danaher, of Connecticut, terminating all the trade agreements six months after the war, was rejected by a vote of 51 to 33. This was four votes more than the opposition of one-third plus one, which is sufficient to damn any treaty. The amendment of Senator Joseph C. O'Mahoney, of Wyoming, requiring all future trade agreements to be ratified by a majority vote in both houses of Congress—a proposal that would have destroyed the entire system of trade agreements through resort to logrolling—was defeated by a vote of 50 to 31. The third amendment by Senator Francis Maloney, of Connecticut, demanding ratification of all agreements under the two-thirds rule in the Senate was defeated by a vote of 44 to 33.

These votes were taken after Harrison Spangler, Chairman of the Republican National Committee, had declared his opposition to placing curbs on the Trade Agreements. The opponents of the Trade Agreements Act, however, were still able to muster more than a one-third minority in their attempt to impair the efficacy of the act. Their tactics show how formidable this minority, under the two-thirds rule, could be in any assault upon a peace treaty. The recrudescence of isolationism would, of course, be fatal to the treaty, and all the more so in case the opposition to the treaty used Lodge's indirect device of destroying a treaty by amendments and reservations.

The list of Democrats opposed to the peace treaty under discussion is probably too large. When party leaders crack the whip, a few of these Senators would finally support the President. But present evidence points to the likelihood that a sufficient number of Democrats would join the Republican irreconcilables to keep the opposition well above the one-third vote that would mean the death sentence of the treaty.

The votes of Senators on all kinds of measures are generally determined by one or more of several incentives. The factors governing senatorial behavior are: (1) the program and tactics of the political party to which the Senator belongs, (2) the demands of constituents and pressure groups, (3) the urgent recommendations of vested interests, (4) newspaper publicity, (5) personal prejudice, bias, or attitude, and (6) objective study of the measure in question.

These incentives have differing weights with different Senators. Party motives are probably stronger than is generally supposed. There are Republican Senators who will oppose any treaty negotiated by a Democratic President; and *vice versa* there are Democratic Senators who would vote against the very same treaty, if negotiated by a Republican President. Deplorable as it may seem, party politics does not stop at the boundary line of the country. No political party is willing for another party to gain the credit for a great achievement. Thus, to the detriment of the welfare of their country, parties will oppose for the sake of opposing.

In the field of foreign policy during the past decade, there is ground for the belief that party politics and personal prejudices surpassed all others as determining factors of senatorial votes, while objective study of the measure in question was probably the weakest. Very few members of the Senate are students of economics, political science, or sociology. Still fewer, like Senator Elbert D. Thomas, of Utah, attend the sessions of learned societies. In the period before Pearl Harbor, the voice of constituents and pressure groups in the field of foreign relations had been divided. The same was true of the newspapers and Big Business. Other than in the tariff and immigration issues, the great vested interests in the United States have not been moved as units either to approve or to oppose American participation in international co-operation. If they were so moved, certain Senators would immediately respond. As a result of divided counsels prior to Pearl Harbor, senatorial votes on foreign policy seem to have been determined in a large measure by party considerations and by personal attitudes.

There is one other personal aspect of senatorial behavior that is worth an appraisal. How far would the vote on the Peace Treaty be guided by the attitude of Senators toward various foreign countries? The upper chamber has seldom been free from Senators who possess a dual mental allegiance. A sentimental interest in the country from which his forefathers have come is not an uncommon nor undesirable trait of any American citizen. With this interest, however, often is associated a traditional hatred of some alleged oppressor of the land of his forebears. These feelings are particularly strong with the Irish-Americans. Persons with a pro-Irish and anti-British complex do not appraise our foreign policy strictly in terms of the welfare of the United States. As members of Congress they have the tendency to oppose any American participation in an international organization in which the United States would be called upon to collaborate with the British Empire. The influence of these personal prejudices on American foreign policy is greater than most Americans suppose.

The career of Senator David I. Walsh, of Massachusetts, is a case in point. Although born in the United States, he comes from Irish stock that cherishes an implacable hatred of Great Britain. In 1919, although a Democrat, he did not hesitate to embarrass President Wilson during the Paris Peace Conference by his demands for Irish independence. His antagonism to Britain made him a bitter opponent of the League of Nations and a supporter of the Lodge maneuvers to destroy the Covenant. Twenty years later, the same anti-British prejudice led him into violent opposition to the Roosevelt policy of aid to Britain. During the debates over the Atlantic patrol system in 1941, he went so far as to attack the President for membership in the Protestant Episcopal Church. One may reasonably expect Senator Walsh to oppose the United Nations, as he opposed the League of Nations in 1919.

The evidence regarding the Senate indicates the probability of another defeat for the peace system in case the constitution of the United Nations, in the form of a treaty, is submitted to the Senate for consent to ratification. International co-operation requires the ratification and execution of agreements negotiated in good faith. The two-thirds rule, permitting the veto of treaties by a minority in the Senate, destroys international co-operation and constitutes a menace to the foreign policy of this country. With the two-thirds rule in effect, our treaty-making procedure is utterly unworkable. If constitutional reform by amendment is impossible, the President and the majority in Congress will be compelled to seek other constitutional methods that will serve as substitutes for treaties.

CHAPTER SEVEN

CAN THE PRESIDENT AND CONGRESS BE PARTNERS?

IN the words of Vice-President Henry A. Wallace, we live in the century of the common man. With equal truth, millions of soldiers and workers believe that this World War is a people's war. The peoples of the democratic states, threatened by the menace of Fascist dictatorship, have risen in their own defense. It remains to be seen, however, whether victory will bring a people's peace.

A people's peace requires: (1) that the universal settlement should promote exclusively the interests of the common man, and (2) that he should share in the making of this fundamental agreement. The first need will be met if the principles of the Four Freedoms and the Atlantic Charter are given force in the peace treaties; the second may never be realized unless constitutional government in not a few countries undergoes some change.

Why should the common man share in the making of the peace and the creation of a new postwar world? The ideology of National Socialism maintains that these matters must be left to the superior judgment of the *Führer*, the leader of the people. Most Americans reject this view. Without indulging in the luxury of self-analysis, they unconsciously accept the tenets of the political philosophy of Jeremy Bentham. With the British Utilitarians, they assume that government exists for the promotion of the greatest happiness of the greatest number. Even more than this, they assume with Bentham that the common man is the best judge of his own happiness. If this assumption be sound, then the common man has a right to participate not only in national government, but also in international organization for social control.

The grinding necessity of the family of nations has compelled the democratic countries to undertake a collective foreign policy. The new international administration, although entirely within the states system, will intimately touch the life of the common man in every nation on this planet. The commitments of the member states in the United Nations will affect the wages, hours, and labor conditions of his employment. They will determine the standard of living that he enjoys, the taxes he pays, and the length of his military service. They will be the reason for the sacrifices he may be called upon to make in the rationing of food and clothing, as a part of a program to prevent the kind of war that grows out of unemployment, starvation, or frustration of desperate peoples.

Decisions of far-reaching character will needs be made by the member states of the United Nations. Here are some of them: How far should the principles of the Atlantic Charter regarding the right of all people to choose their form of government be applied if Soviet Russia insists on the sovietization of East Poland and the Baltic states? Should the United Nations seek to offset possible sovietization of Germany by Russo-German forces? If the control of Soviet Russia engulfs Germany and even France, then Great Britain is left face to face with a possibly hostile continent. In that case, how far is it wise to extend the American-British commitments?

What policy should guide the United Nations regarding the reconstruction of self-government in Germany? Is it prudent to insist on the breakup of Prussia as a political unit in the new Germany? How far is it expedient to encourage a Central European Confederation? Should Germany be excluded from such a confederation?

What should be the limits of the defeated Japanese Empire? Can markets be opened for Japanese goods that will give continued employment to the millions of Japanese workers? Starvation and national frustration, the common man now has learned, are among the causes of war. How far should the United Nations go in urging the government of Generalissimo Chiang Kai-shek to keep peace with the millions of Chinese Communists? Such a policy might prevent a civil war in China that would again threaten the stability of the Far East; but, the persuasion of the Kuomintang to adopt this policy might require commitments that would increase the tax burden of the common man.

These are only a few of the urgent questions that must be answered by the United Nations. The decisions, whatever they may be, will affect the daily life of the common man in the United States and every other member state of the United Nations. Undoubtedly, the willingness of the average citizen to make sacrifices for the execution of these decisions will depend upon his consciousness of personal participation in the selection of the policies to be pursued.

Alexander Pope showed a small understanding of modern government when he penned the oft-quoted lines—

> For forms of government let fools contest;
> Whate'er is best administered is best.

If the form of government is democratic, then political organization is of prime importance. In the postwar age, the democracies will be called upon to repair the havoc wrought by authoritarian and totalitarian dictatorships. The completeness of the common man's identification with the organs of democratic government will largely determine the degree of efficiency brought to the gigantic task of reconstructing the world. The momentum of public opinion will be the indispensable requisite for its achievement.

There are some critics of American politics who hold that the principle of the separation of powers is a fatal obstacle to the efficiency of our government. Admittedly, the presidential form of government has some defects which do not appear in a parliamentary system such as that of Great Britain. There, the Prime Minister is the choice of the majority of the House of Commons. He is Prime Minister only because of this fact. A vote of nonconfidence in the House of Commons causes his immediate resignation or a general election in which the electorate decides which of the two or three political parties shall control Parliament.

Further, the Prime Minister and his colleagues in the cabinet are responsible for drafting most of the bills passed by Parliament, and in turn, they administer these same bills in the form of statutes. The failure of the House of Commons to approve any of the bills of the cabinet will cause its resignation or a general election. Under this system, in which cabinets have an average age of about four years, friction between the executive and the legislature is reduced to a minimum. Not even a general election is required to change a cabinet. In 1940, after the German invasion of Norway, when Parliament was ready to move from a weak to a strong war policy, Prime Minister Neville Chamberlain with no fuss at all gave way to Winston Churchill.

Under a presidential system such as in the United States, the Chief Executive is elected by the people for a term of four years and holds office independently of the legislature. Representatives are elected for two-year terms, and Senators for six-year terms, one-third of the Senate being elected every two years. Under the principle of separation of powers, Congress has the function of the enactment of laws, and the President, of the enforcement of laws. The President also possesses the power to initiate and largely direct foreign policy, although the Senate, through the veto of his treaties, has a negative control of foreign policy. The President may recommend legislation to Congress, while Congress may, in turn, seek to curb his administration by restrictive provisions in statutes.

Obviously, bitter contests can develop between the President and an unwilling Congress. It is even possible for the President and either house of Congress to be of opposing political parties, as in the last two years of Taft's administration and the last two years of Wilson's second administration. The harmony between the executive and the legislature in Great Britain exists by virtue of the fact that the Prime Minister is the choice of the majority in Parliament and is completely responsible to Parliament. The friction between the President and Congress is due to the fact that leadership and responsibility are divided.

Prolonged contests between the President and Congress give the voters a profound sense of frustration. The President is the representative of all the people. Congress is composed of members who represent the people within the four hundred odd Congressional districts and the forty-eight States. Thus, a stalemate between the two groups of officials who represent him in the national capitol leaves the common man in a bewildered frame of mind. It even leads him to distrust his government.

The average American's sense of participation in government is probably much greater than generally supposed. The voter whose candidate has won the presidential election possesses in most cases a continuing pride in the sagacity of his choice. Independents who desire sound policy and efficient administration regardless of party politics congratulate themselves on the achievements of the President in these fields. Citizens who write letters, send telegrams, sign petitions, and otherwise express their opinions in an effort to influence the White House, are even more conscious of sharing in the act of governing. The same relationship obtains between large groups of voters and their respective Representatives and Senators. From these representatives—both executive and legislative—their constituents expect effective action. In such citizens, a deadlock between the President and Congress evokes impatience bordering upon disgust.

It will serve no purpose here to enter the controversy over parliamentary versus presidential government. The aim of this book is to show the necessity for a constitutional amendment to abolish the two-thirds rule and the monopoly of the Senate over the approval of treaties. It will not be out of place, however, to suggest a few measures which, without destroying the principle of separation of power, ought to promote co-operation between the President and Congress in the field of foreign policy.

Co-operation between the President and Congress moves like a pendulum. Sometimes it swings to a position in which Congress allows the White House to draft the bills which it docilely enacts as statutes. At other times, the pendulum swings to the other extreme in which Congress rejects any executive participation in the framing of legislation, and attempts to put the administration into a legal straitjacket. After the "bank holiday" in 1933, Congress mildly permitted the executive to draft the text of the emergency statutes—the first acts of the New Deal—which it speedily adopted. Later, as the economic crisis passed, the pendulum swung the other way, and Congress balked at the leadership of the President. In war, as in any other national emergency, Congress follows the President, who is indeed the Commander-in-Chief. But with the coming of peace, Congress again moves toward independence, and even opposition.

The first session of the Seventy-eighth Congress, which convened in January, 1943, gave signs of an attempt to reject the leadership of the President even before the termination of hostilities with the Axis powers. In domestic policy, Congress showed its hand by the dissolution of the National Resources Planning Board. So bent was Congress upon ousting the presidential leadership in social research that it forbade the use of any monies in any other appropriation bill for the revival of the Board. The deep-seated antipathy to the Board's plans was expressed by Senator Robert A. Taft, of Ohio, who branded them as "partly socialism and partly the product of a dangerous imagination." Before its activities were liquidated, however, the Board issued its "cradle-to-grave" Security Plan. It was almost completely ignored by Congress, which gave more attention to the British Beveridge Report than it deigned to confer on the American project.

At the same time, the educational (propaganda, if you prefer) activities of the Office of War Information in the United States were drastically curtailed. The President was not to be permitted to advertise his peace plans to the American people through the agency headed by the distinguished commentator, Elmer Davis.

After a partisan attempt on the part of a small group of Republican Congressmen to strangle the Hull Trade Agreements, in June, 1943, Congress extended the authority of the President to continue the crusade for the leveling of tariff barriers to foreign trade. The act limited the President's authority to two years, whereas each of the previous acts named three years. Nevertheless, the passage of the act marked the nearest approach that Congress made to expressing its views on postwar foreign policy. Even here, the House was far ahead of the Senate in the support of international co-operation. The vote in the House on the Trade Agreements Act was 342 to 65 in favor of the measure; in the Senate it was 59 to 23.

In the meantime, Congress showed a disposition to make its own study of postwar reconstruction in both the domestic and the international fields. In February, 1943, Senator Walter F. George, of Georgia, chairman of the Finance Committee, called for a joint Congressional committee authorized to plan a postwar economic program. A month later, the announcement of the Keynes plan for international currency stabilization, backed by the British Exchequer, followed by the publication of the White plan, backed by the U. S. Treasury Department, showed that the executive branch was still far ahead of the legislature in monetary research.

On March 24, 1943, the Senate Committee on Foreign Relations made a decision that was destined to have far-reaching results. Unanimously, it appointed a subcommittee to study all resolutions on postwar settlements and co-operation with the United Nations.

All of these events showed the determination of Congress to write the postwar Charter for America, as well as a growing inclination to guide the peace settlement.

Throughout the spring and summer of 1943, the President and Congress maneuvered for position in postwar planning. The American people were totally unaware of the struggle, and even less of its significance. The spectacular finish of the North African campaign, the invasion of Sicily, and the victories of General MacArthur in the South Pacific riveted the attention of the people on the progress of the war. The defiance of law by John L. Lewis and the United Mine Workers' Union, the increase in the income tax, the rationing of food and clothing, and the controversy over the drafting of fathers absorbed almost all of their remaining attention. Not even every member of Congress understood the swiftly moving trend in the relations of the President and Congress.

Great issues were at stake. In internal policy, the President hoped to preserve the New Deal in the postwar Charter for America. In foreign policy, he was determined to keep the interfering hand of the isolationists out of the peace settlement. In this the President had a special advantage. His predictions of the menace of the Axis powers had proved to be correct. The opponents of his attempt to defend the Americas had been discredited. His personal prestige was expanded with every American victory in Africa, Europe, and Asia, and his picture was now roundly cheered in motion-picture houses, where two years previously it had been hissed. Popular support of his plans for American participation in the peace system was overwhelming. Even the isolationists sourly admitted this fact.

At the same time, the reputation of his Secretary of State added support to the President's position. Cordell Hull, now seventy-two years of age, had presided over the Department of State for ten years—a longer period of service than any of his illustrious predecessors. He is one of the greatest in a long list of distinguished Secretaries. Having served in Congress from 1907 to 1933, the Secretary was familiar with every phase of Congressional behavior. He enjoyed a friendly acquaintance with a larger number of Senators and Representatives than any previous head of the Department, with the possible exception of William Jennings Bryan.

As spokesman of the American people in foreign affairs, President Roosevelt held the odds against Congress. The Atlantic Charter and the Declaration of the United Nations had captured the imagination of the common man. These were his achievements. Every address after each of his historic conferences with Prime Minister Churchill strengthened his leadership. Despite all these advantages, however, the Department of State was apprehensive. Officials recalled the destruction of the Wilsonian peace system in 1919-1920; and were fully aware that Wheeler, Nye, Clark, Taft, Willis, Aiken, Danaher, Walsh, Hiram Johnson, and other unregenerate isolationists in the Senate were saving their strength and cunning to destroy any permanent alliance with the United Nations. Not so the American people, who confidently expected that the President would find a way to give life to the Atlantic Charter—he was a politician with a marvelous bag of tricks.

In Congress, the isolationists were silenced, for the moment, by the stupendous events of global war. Congressional opinion on foreign policy was largely a reflection of the President's peace aims. The President, however, could not forget the bitter contest with the isolationists in the period immediately preceding Pearl Harbor. The greater number of the Senators who had at that time been most active in attacking his policy of aid to Britain still retained their seats in the Senate. Many of them were his personal enemies. There was no evidence that they had abated a whit of their isolationism. They scoffed at the Atlantic Charter, sneered at the Four Freedoms, and cast doubts on the United Nations. There was every expectation that at the end of the war they would seek to sabotage the peace system. Naturally, the President was determined to keep as much of the planning for the United Nations as possible out of reach of their destructive hands.

All these facts account for the reluctance of President Roosevelt to support the Ball-Hatch Resolution. This resolution (S. Res. 114) was introduced in the Senate on March 9, 1943, by Senators Joseph H. Ball (Minnesota), Lister Hill (Alabama), Harold H. Burton (Ohio) and Carl A. Hatch (New Mexico). Two of the sponsors were Republicans and two were Democrats.

Couched in admirably selected phrases, the resolution of the four Senators reads as follows:

Resolved, That the Senate advises that the United States take the initiative in calling meetings of representatives of the United Nations for the purpose of forming an organization of the United Nations with specific and limited authority—

(1) To assist in co-ordinating and fully utilizing the military and economic resources of all member nations in the prosecution of the war against the Axis.

(2) To establish temporary administrations for Axis-controlled areas of the world as these are occupied by United Nations forces, until such time as permanent governments can be established.

(3) To administer relief and assistance in economic rehabilitation in territories of member nations needing such aid and in Axis territory occupied by United Nations forces.

(4) To establish procedures and machinery for peaceful settlement of disputes and disagreements between nations.

(5) To provide for the assembly and maintenance of a United Nations military force and to suppress by immediate use of such force any future attempt at military aggression by any nation.

That the Senate further advises that any establishment of such United Nations organization provide machinery for its modification, for the delegation of additional specific and limited functions to such organization, and for admission of other nations to membership, and that member nations should commit themselves to seek no territorial aggrandizement.

The Ball-Hatch Resolution bore the mark of statesmanship. A prudent regard for the future required that Congress commit itself to a policy for the joint administration of occupied territory, the maintenance of an international police force, a program of foreign relief and rehabilitation, and constitutional government for the United Nations. Undoubtedly, the resolution had the support of the majority of the American people. So far, so good. But in the Department of State the resolution brought a sharp difference of opinion. Undersecretary Sumner Welles thought it would prove helpful for Congress to go on record concerning the shape of the peace. Secretary Hull feared that public debate would play into the hands of isolationist Senators and insisted that the peace should be left to the management of the professional diplomats.

Under the shadow of the Senate monopoly of treaty ratification, both views offered risks and gains. As soon as the Ball-Hatch Resolution was introduced in the Senate, reactionary members offered amendments that invited the sabotage of the future peace system by a repetition of the defeat of the Covenant of the League of Nations. Among others was the amendment offered by the unrelenting isolationist, Senator Raymond E. Willis, of Indiana, providing that any agreements made under authority conferred by the Ball-Hatch Resolution would not be binding on the United States without the assent of two-thirds of the Senators present.

Equally reactionary was the resolution (S. Res. 91) introduced on February 4, 1943, by the isolationist Senator Gillette, of Iowa. This innocent-looking proposal approved the Atlantic Charter and the Declaration of the United Nations. In that respect it harmonized with public opinion. The destructive aspect of the resolution lay in the fact that it indirectly barred the President from negotiating any peace settlement based upon executive agreements. It would compel the Chief Executive to use only the treaty form for all pacts creating the new agencies of the United Nations. It would place the peace at the mercy of a one-third minority in an upper chamber that has notoriously lagged behind public opinion in the great crisis of democracy.

As bait for unwary supporters of the peace system, Senator Gillette later introduced a proposal to amend the Constitution by substituting a majority vote of the Senate for the approval of treaties in place of the two-thirds rule. He failed, however, to allude to the fact that there was no binding connection between S. Res. 91, which would force the hand of the Chief Executive, and the proposed amendment for the abolition of the two-thirds rule. Under the Gillette plan, if the proposed amendment failed of adoption, the President would still be compelled to submit the peace treaties to the tender mercies of a minority of the Senate.

More compatible with the strategy of the White House was the concurrent resolution (H. Con. Res. 25) introduced in the House of Representatives by Dr. J. William Fulbright, of Arkansas. In the simplest of legislative language, the resolution read: "Resolved by the House of Representatives (the Senate concurring) that Congress hereby expresses itself as favoring the creation of appropriate international machinery with power adequate to establish and to maintain a just and lasting peace among the nations of the world, and as favoring participation of the United States therein." This resolution, introduced by one of the most scholarly members of Congress (Dr. Fulbright was formerly president of the University of Arkansas), received, on June 15, 1943, the unanimous approval of the Committee on Foreign Affairs. Both Republicans and Democrats on this Committee voted to report it favorably to the House.

The Fulbright Resolution, while in line with public opinion, also had the advantage of offering a basis of co-operation between the President and Congress. Some members of Congress held that the resolution even afforded sufficient authorization for the negotiation of a peace settlement in the form of an executive agreement rather than a treaty. The adoption of the resolution—a concurrent rather than a joint resolution—required a two-thirds vote of both houses of Congress. Its passage, therefore, would give some indication of the chances for approval of the definitive peace treaty by the Senate. In September, when Congress reconvened after the summer recess, the House Committee on Foreign Affairs weakly surrendered to Senator Vandenberg's *constitutionalism* and amended the Fulbright Resolution by the addition of the words: *through its constitutional processes.* This provision, it was said, would make the resolution more palatable to Republicans. In its amended form, the resolution was adopted by the House of Representatives by a vote of 360 to 29, while 41 members refrained from voting. The vote showed that more than two-thirds of the lower chamber approved in principle the Roosevelt-Churchill peace pattern.

The Fulbright Resolution was received by members of the Senate Committee on Foreign Relations with studied coolness. Indeed, Senator Connally moved to postpone all consideration of postwar peace aims on the ground that public debate at that time would injure the solidarity of the United Nations. This lame excuse which was brushed aside by a word from the President welcoming an expression of Congressional sentiment, failed to hide the resentment of numerous Senators over the initiation of a pronouncement on foreign policy by the lower chamber.

Popular comment on the situation was against the Senate. The House of Representatives had waited twenty-one months for a Senatorial expression of postwar aims. Public opinion as well as diplomatic strategy demanded an expression of Congressional opinion on this subject. The lower house, after deferring to the Senate, had at last spoken in accord with this public opinion. Assertion of the prestige of the Senate by resentful Senators at this critical time boded little good for the final peace settlement.

Both Congress and the Department of State are aware of the danger of attempting to solve twentieth century international problems with eighteenth century diplomatic methods. The State Department would meet the situation by relying on executive agreements, thus keeping all pacts out of the grasp of the Senate. The isolationists in Congress would solve the problem by a strict interpretation of the Constitution, compelling the President to submit every agreement to the Senate. Moderate supporters of the peace system in Congress think the solution lies in the adoption of some method for the participation of both houses of Congress in the authorization of commitments, if not the approval of all fundamental agreements.

Much of the recent criticism of the Department comes from observers who see a tendency in the Department to monopolize the control of foreign affairs. Robert Bendiner, in *The Riddle of the State Department* (1942), describes the Department as full of officials whose chief aim in life is to keep Congressional control out of the field of foreign policy. Critics fear that, trading upon the enormous prestige of President Roosevelt and Secretary Hull, the Department will seek to carry off the negotiations of the peace settlement without any consultation with Congress.

The fear is partly justified. Secretary Hull presides over a Department that resents interference from Capitol Hill. Although the Secretary himself served twenty-two years in the House of Representatives and four years in the Senate, he now takes the Departmental rather than the Congressional view.

There is reason for career officers in the Department to resent the advice of Senators. The Senate contains an inordinate number of narrowly trained lawyers. They have a penchant for rendering ponderous advice on subjects in which their competence is not extensive. These men cannot see the text of an agreement without wishing to revise it, to "improve" it, as they say.

Regardless of their lack of information or experience, they are not satisfied unless they have tinkered with the phraseology of every sentence. Usually trained only in the Anglo-Saxon legal system, they fussily attempt to reduce the text of an agreement to the routine of the American law schools.

Quibbling over legalistic niceties in a document which accurately reflects the agreement of negotiators whom the Senators have never met, least of all conversed with, is almost the negation of diplomacy. It means the reopening of negotiations with the foreign diplomats; it risks reaching no agreement at all. Thus, the very sight of a Senator causes many career men in the State Department to hide their carefully negotiated agreements more closely in their portfolios.

On their side, Senators grumble about the secrecy of the Department of State. Not only is the Senate not consulted, but also it is not even informed of the President's foreign policy. The Department of State, they say, is the only department that does not issue an annual report.

The Secretary of State tells Senators who complain that the Senate receives too little information on foreign affairs that any Senator is at liberty to come to his office and read, in confidence, the foreign dispatches. Senators who suggest a closer liaison between the Senate and the State Department during the negotiation of treaties are told that the Secretary constantly consults many members of the Senate and the House of Representatives. He reminds Senators that, under the Constitution, the President is entrusted with the conduct of foreign relations, and that each house has a respective function to perform in co-operation with the presidential policy.

Toward the proposal of a Foreign Relations Advisory Council, the Secretary has shown a suave contempt. The creation of this body was proposed by Senator Alexander Wiley late in 1942. The Council which he suggested was to consist of the Secretary of State, the Undersecretary, other members of the Department, to be chosen by the Secretary, the chairman and the ranking minority member of the Senate Committee on Foreign Relations, the chairman and the ranking minority member of the House Committee on Foreign Affairs, and such other Senators as the President might from time to time designate.

Secretary Hull's answer to the Wiley Resolution was exactly what, in view of its source, might have been expected. The Wisconsin Senator is the type of pettifogging lawyer that the Department deeply distrusts. In addition, he is a reactionary isolationist. His voting record, in the days before Pearl Harbor, shows consistent opposition to every major measure of defense against the Axis powers proposed by the Roosevelt administration. He fought the revision of the Neutrality Act of 1937 which proved so very helpful to the Axis powers. He voted against the Selective Service and Training Bill, the Lend-Lease Bill, the extension of the draft, the transfer of Axis ships to American use, the Armed Ship Bill, the Ship Seizure Bill, and the second Lend-Lease Bill. He did his best to limit the use of American armed forces to the Western Hemisphere.

Few voting records in the Senate show less grasp of realities in foreign policy than that of the Wisconsin Senator. It is thus not surprising that the Department of State viewed his proposal as an attempt by a confirmed isolationist to hamstring American participation in planning the new world peace.

Secretary Hull, in his polite but cold reply to the Wiley Resolution, pointed to the already existing Senate Committee on Foreign Relations and the House Committee on Foreign Affairs. He called attention to the frequent appearance of the Secretary and other officials of the Department of State before these committees. If either house, he said, desired to alter this method of hearing and questioning the Secretary of State, it was at liberty, of course, to amend its own rules. But, as for the Secretary, he intended to respect the constitutional doctrine of the separation of powers.

Dissident Senators are far from satisfied by these replies. They retort that the Secretary's advisers in the Senate are limited to the friends of the administration. The counsels of isolationist Senators are seldom, if ever, sought. It is suspected that the only procedural change which would be welcomed by the Secretary is the substitution of executive agreements for the old style treaty. But this is the nightmare of many an isolationist. Senators know all too well that if treaties were abandoned in favor of executive agreements, the Senate would be relegated to the same position as the House of Representatives in treaty-making. Deprived of its exalted power of rejecting or approving treaties, the upper chamber would retain only the more humble function of participating, with the House of Representatives, in the enactment of appropriation bills and other measures for the purpose of fulfilling the obligations of executive conventions.

Abolition of the two-thirds rule and of the Senate monopoly of ratification of treaties would lead to greater co-operation between Congress and the President in matters of foreign policy. At present, the State Department, in its fear of veto of international acts by a minority of the Senate, is uncommunicative and eager to by-pass Congress. Obversely, Congressional suspicions that the Department is pursuing a secret policy breeds obstruction. It is a vicious circle of distrust, secrecy, suspicion and opposition. If the control of American foreign policy is to be democratized, the approval of treaties will have to be transferred to majority rule in both houses of Congress. Until this democratic reform is accomplished, American treaty procedure will remain dangerously archaic.

Until such a basic reform takes place, however, the conduct of foreign relations can probably be somewhat improved through closer contact between the President and Congress. Although the complaint regarding lack of information comes chiefly from Senators who suspect that the President is pursuing, without public announcement, a policy of which they may disapprove, it also comes from Senators who loyally support the Administration. All parties and groups in both houses of Congress would welcome a more adequate system of information and consultation.

The new alliance with Great Britain in the battle

for democracy, and the immense popularity of Winston Churchill in America have turned the eyes of this nation toward a form of government that can wage war with such vigor and produce such magnificent leadership. Even the Senate is a little infected with this admiration of the British parliamentary system. Senators who have cast bitter aspersions on British foreign policy in the last few years are now calling attention to the advantages of the cabinet system as practiced in Britain.

There is no doubt that under the parliamentary form of government information is more readily obtained from the cabinet than under the presidential system. The Prime Minister, as a member of Parliament, cannot use his high office as a barrier between himself and his fellow members. He, along with the rest of the cabinet, reports at frequent intervals to the House of Commons. These reports may be followed by protracted debates. In addition, an early part of each daily sitting of the House of Commons is devoted to questions. The Prime Minister, the Secretary of State for Foreign Affairs, or an undersecretary will answer any question on foreign affairs unless it is deemed incompatible with the public interest to give a reply.

The American counterpart to the British question time is the press conference. Several times a week, the President receives newspapermen at the White House. For the past two decades it has been customary for the Secretary of State also to hold a daily press conference. Informing of the public is a prerequisite of democracy. But there is a tendency in Congress to resent the press conference on the ground that by this means the President informs the country on matters which should in the first instance be laid before Congress. Furthermore, the President can more easily dodge the questions of newspapermen, if he is so inclined, than can the British Prime Minister evade the interrogations of members of Parliament.

When the Prime Minister speaks in the House of Commons he stands in front of his seat on the Treasury Bench. Facing him, across the aisle, and sitting on the Front Opposition Bench, is the Leader of His Majesty's Opposition. This statesman is the member of Parliament who will be summoned by the Crown to form a new ministry in case he succeeds in defeating the present cabinet. This fact tempers his criticism of the Prime Minister; for if the tide of politics puts him in the place of the Premier tomorrow he may find it necessary, for the welfare of his country, to advocate the same policy as that of the defeated ministry.

Critics of American government have frequently claimed that some of the admirable features of parliamentary government can be adopted in America, without abandoning the doctrine of separation of powers. Undoubtedly, American foreign policy would be more consistently clarified if, day after day, Wendell Willkie (now titular leader of the Republican Party and thus leader of the opposition) sat face to face with President Roosevelt. Or if, day after day, Secretary Hull were required to answer the questions of Governor Harold E. Stassen or Senator Joseph H. Ball, or any other possible successor to his office. The parliamentary system, however, is one form of government and the presidential another form, and never can the twain meet while they retain their identities.

Inasmuch as the President holds the dual role of presiding officer of the state and Chief Executive, he cannot logically be a member of the legislature or in daily attendance in the legislature. He does come before Congress at the opening of each session of Congress and on strategic occasions to read his message in person. Some of the leading pronouncements on American foreign policy, from the Monroe Doctrine in 1822 to the Four Freedoms in 1941, have been contained in addresses by the President to Congress. But this is as far as presidential participation within the halls of Congress can consistently go.

The case is somewhat different with cabinet officers. For many years it has been proposed that the heads of departments should have seats in both houses of Congress. By changing the rules of the Senate and the House of Representatives, cabinet officers could take seats in Congress without resorting to a constitutional amendment. They could have the right to participate in debate, but not to vote. Under such an arrangement, its proponents claim, the Secretary of State would not have to attend every session of both houses of Congress, and he could appear in either house to address Congress or to submit himself to the questions of the members at his discretion.

The proposal for granting Congressional seats to cabinet officers is a superficial answer to an old problem. So long as the presidential system is retained, cabinet seats in Congress are a futile gesture. The reason is plain. The Secretary of State owes no responsibility to Congress. If, in the course of debate, members of Congress seek to wring commitments from him, the legislature encroaches upon the rights of the Chief Executive. If he speaks merely as an agent, his participation in Congress tends to decline to routine announcements.

Any tendency toward permitting the Secretary of State to commit the Chief Executive in debates in Congress would be a major disaster to the presidential system. It would diminish the prestige of the President and impair his efficient direction of national policy. The leadership of the President is the essential virtue of the presidential system. With the exception of the Vice-President, his successor in case of death, the President is the only national officer elected by all of the electorate. The achievement of the national program depends upon the quality of his leadership. Any impairment of his opportunity to lead the nation would impede the operation of national policy and would promote confusion, division and delay in national decisions.

But the problem of information and consultation remains to be solved. As a matter of fact, it is on the way to solution, first by means of the expanding publication program of the Department of State, and second, by means of the conferences of the Secretary and members of Congress, such as those which in the summer of 1943 resulted in the proposal of the Green-Sayre formula.

It is possible that the publication of an annual report by the Department of State would prove of assistance. The Department already publishes a weekly *Bulletin* giving a mass of detail about the Department. Selections from the diplomatic correspondence are published in the yearly volumes of *Foreign Relations*, although these volumes are now far behind the current year. Numerous reports on international conferences and other activities are issued from time to time. Paradoxical as it may seem, Congress is reluctant to appropriate funds for more extensive publication by the State Department of information on foreign affairs.

The timing of State Department documents is not so effective as the needs of democracy demand. The Department issued, in January, 1943, a publication: *Peace and War: United States Foreign Policy, 1931-1941*. This admirable account of how war came to America appeared thirteen months after Pearl Harbor. It should have been issued in the first month of the war.

In a classic of the antebellum days, the amazing *American White Paper: The Story of American Diplomacy and the Second World War*, two newspaper correspondents, Alsop and Kintner, say that while the President and the Secretary propose and the Senate finally disposes, after all it is neither the President nor the Secretary nor the Senate that really makes American foreign policy. Rather, the cables make it. In other words, the dispatches coming in day by day, week by week, from American diplomatic and consular agents in every capital and commercial center of the world relate facts which eventually determine our foreign policy, regardless of isolationists or internationalists, whether in the White House or in the Senate.

Officials in the Department of State cynically classify all Senators as those who read and those who do not read the dispatches. Senators can obtain, in confidence, any information in possession of the Department of State simply on making a request of the Secretary of State. Such information, however, may not be made the basis of a public statement or an attack on the presidential policy. For this reason, some Senators refuse to seek any confidential information. There are, indeed, Senators, like the late William E. Borah, who believe that they know as much about world events as the dispatch-reading officials in the State Department. There are others who think their "hunches" are superior to the judgments of the career officers in the Foreign Service.

Under the presidential system, the biparty conference between the President, his Secretary of State and members of Congress is almost the only method for insuring co-operation in the conduct of foreign affairs. It is astonishing that this technique has not been more frequently employed. There have been instances when conferences of this character have proved futile. In February, 1919, while the Paris Peace Congress was in session, President Wilson returned to the United States partly to confer with the Senate Committee on Foreign Relations and the House Committee on Foreign Affairs. In the conference, held in the East Room of the White House, following a dinner given to the members, the President submitted to a most rigorous questioning by members of the Committees. Again, in August, after the Treaty of Versailles had been transmitted to the Senate, the President met with the Senate Committee on Foreign Relations.

In the summer of 1939, when President Roosevelt was urging repeal of some of the provisions of the Neutrality Act, he invited leaders of both political parties to the White House. Secretary Hull and other officials of the Department of State were also present. It was on this occasion that Senator Borah declared that he possessed better information than the Department of State regarding events in Europe. Many Senators took Borah at his word, in spite of the fact that the Department has a Foreign Service of several thousand officials in every capital in the world who continually cable their dispatches. This conference was no more successful than President Wilson's had been.

However, the success of the series of conferences between the Secretary of State and the subcommittee of the Senate Committee on Foreign Relations in the summer of 1943 suggests the probable usefulness of periodic conferences (once a month, or oftener) between the President, his Secretary of State, and the leaders of both parties in Congress. Such conferences, if they are to be effective, should not be limited to the chairmen and ranking minority member of the Senate Committee on Foreign Relations and of the House Committee on Foreign Affairs, but should also include the majority and minority leaders of both houses. In this experiment in partnership between the President and Congress, Senators would have the advantage of access to confidential information without the embarrassment of making requests upon the Secretary. At the same time, the President would have an opportunity to learn the attitude of Congressmen who do not see eye-to-eye with him in foreign policy.

All of these devices may be helpful in promoting a genuine partnership between the President and Congress. But such a partnership can never take place between a democratic President and an autocratic minority in the Senate. It is hopeless to expect much improvement in the co-operation of the President and Congress in foreign affairs without the fundamental reform of abolishing, by constitutional amendment, the two-thirds rule and the monopoly of the Senate over the consent to ratification of treaties.

CHAPTER EIGHT

WE CAN AND MUST AMEND THE CONSTITUTION

ARGUMENTS in favor of amending the treaty-making process of the American Constitution can be reduced to two basic propositions: (1) The present process of ratification permits the will of the American people to be flagrantly ignored. (2) It is a menace to world peace.

There are persons even in America who believe that the will of the people may be flouted year after year by minority controls. They avoid discussion of this question in election campaigns, but at other times they advance the doctrine often in some sort of disguise. The argument that the will of the people ought to be thwarted by minority rule is exactly the ground upon which Senators must stand who object to the abolition of the Senate monopoly of the process of ratification of treaties.

The dangers of too frequent evasion of the Constitution have already been discussed. But it is necessary to examine the further risks incurred by frequent resort to devious ways for circumventing the plain intent of the fundamental law.

In great emergencies, Presidents have occasionally violated the Constitution in order to promote the defense and general welfare of the country. When Thomas Jefferson, in 1803, purchased Louisiana, he

166

was convinced that he was trampling on the Constitution. Nevertheless, in the interest of the nation, he did not hesitate to override the fundamental law. The annexations of Texas and Hawaii by joint resolution, after treaties of annexation had failed in the Senate, were patent attempts to set aside the Constitution in the national interest. Such episodes arouse admiration for the courage and ingenuity of the statesmen who in some measure violated the supreme law in order to promote the welfare of the republic. But they do not contribute to the respect for law which we deem to be one of the essentials of democratic government.

If it be necessary to violate the Constitution in order to set aside an obstreperous minority which seeks to frustrate the will of the nation, bold statesmanship will not hesitate to act in the interest of the republic. But, why should the American people have to resort to indirection, year after year? Why should our government do basely by devious ways what could be done admirably by a straightforward method? In other words, why tolerate in our fundamental law a provision that places a great nation in the humiliating position of dodging the universally accepted method of making contracts with other states?

The Green-Sayre formula for escaping the veto of the isolationist minority in the Senate may be an unpleasant necessity forced upon the nation as a result of a peculiar provision in the Constitution. But this does not mean that statesmen who see the need for honest participation in the United Nations should not seek a permanent solution of this troublesome problem. It is true that the power over approval of treaties cannot be taken from the minority in the Senate without its consent, unless an unusual method of amending the Constitution be employed. A joint resolution for the purpose of proposing an amendment to the Constitution requires a two-thirds vote in both houses. But an appeal to the people of the United States may ultimately lead to a moral revolution that will compel the minority to give way to the public interest. When the American people realize that only a little band of Senators, representing on this question no interest but their own, stand between the people and the fulfillment of the national aspiration, the public pressure upon Congress will be such that few Senators will be able to withstand it.

If even a deeply aroused public opinion fails to move Senators, resort can be had to resolutions from State legislatures. Under Article I of the Constitution, Congress is compelled to call a national convention to propose amendments after receiving the application of the legislatures of two-thirds of the States. The amendments proposed by such a convention become part of the supreme law when ratified by the legislatures or conventions in three-fourths of the States. This procedure has never yet been employed. It is a cumbersome method. But it would at least outflank the obstructing minority in the Senate.

Proposals to amend the treaty-making provision of the Constitution began to be made early in the history of the Union. Amendments of the advice and consent procedure were proposed in the ratifying conventions of Virginia and North Carolina in 1788 and 1789. Far from seeking to make the process more democratic, these proposals sought to render it more in line with the States Rights doctrine. They were not included in the ten proposed amendments which Congress referred to the States in 1789 and which, after ratification, became the first ten amendments of the Constitution. In 1796, the legislature of Virginia proposed the first democratic amendment to the effect "that no treaty containing any stipulation upon the subject of the powers vested in Congress shall become the supreme law of the land until it shall have been approved in those particulars by a majority in the House of Representatives, and that the President before he shall ratify any treaty shall submit the same to the House of Representatives."

As might be expected, it has been the large states like New York, Pennsylvania, and Illinois which have persisted in offering amendments of a democratic character. In 1884, a representative from Illinois proposed that treaties should be ratified by the consent of the House of Representatives as well as of the Senate. In 1899, a similar proposal was made by a representative from Pennsylvania. Between 1919 and 1935, Representative Anthony J. Griffen, of New York, offered six amendments placing consent to ratification in the hands of a majority of the House and Senate.

The record shows only one proposal from a small State for the purpose of democratizing the treaty-making process. This is, of course, to be expected. The "pocket boroughs" of American politics are loath to relinquish their lucrative position in the federal system. Nor has the Senate shown itself to be eager to modernize the ratification process. The first amendment proposed by the Senate appeared during the acrimonious debate over the Covenant of the League of Nations. On March 22, 1920, Senator Robert L. Owen, of Oklahoma, offered a resolution for an amendment providing for ratification of treaties by consent of a majority of the Senate. He renewed this resolution in 1921 and 1923, but all to no avail. Senator James P. Pope, of Idaho, offered a similar amendment in 1935, after the rejection of the Protocol of the World Court, again without results.

In February, 1943, Senator Guy M. Gillette, of Iowa, once more introduced the Owen amendment, calling for the approval of treaties by a majority of the Senators. Subsequently, he introduced three other joint resolutions proposing several other methods of approval of treaties. The amendments proposed by these four joint resolutions read as follows:

S. J. Res. 36. The President shall have power, by and with the advice and consent of the Senate, to make treaties, provided a majority of the Senators concur.

S. J. Res. 37. The President shall have power to make treaties, but no such treaty shall be operative until it has been approved by a majority of the Senators.

S. J. Res. 38. The President shall have power, by and with the advice and consent of the Senate, to make treaties, provided a majority of the Senators and a majority of the members of the House of Representatives concur.

S. J. Res. 52. The President shall have power, by and with the advice of the Senate, to frame treaties, and, with the consent of the Senate, a majority of the Senators present concurring therein, to conclude the same.

These resolutions were in due time submitted to the subcommittee of the Senate Committee on Foreign Relations which had been appointed on March 24, 1943, to study all resolutions relating to postwar settlements. The subcommittee, as already explained, had undertaken a study of the procedure of authorizing and approving postwar pacts as well as proposals such as the Ball-Hatch Resolution for promoting the organization of the United Nations.

What are the merits of the Gillette amendment? Unhappily, they are conspicuously small. The resolution (S. J. Res. 36) would indeed somewhat mitigate the two-thirds rule, but it would still retain the Senate monopoly over the ratification process. Even the two-thirds rule is only slightly relaxed. The Gillette amendment requires the consent of a majority of the total number of Senators, rather than a majority of the Senators present in the Senate chamber for the approval of treaties. To the uninitiated, there may seem to be small difference between the two kinds of majorities. In practice, however, the difference is great. According to usual legislative procedure, the passage of a bill in both houses of Congress requires only a simple majority vote of the members present, if there is a quorum. In both houses, a quorum consists of a majority of the members. In other words, in the Senate, a quorum is forty-nine Senators. Accordingly, a bill passed by a bare majority of a quorum of the Senate would require twenty-five yeas as against twenty-four nays.

Only on the rarest occasions are all Senators present and prepared to cast their votes for any measure. It is true that absentee Senators may be paired under an arrangement whereby the vote of an absentee Senator in favor of a measure is offset by the vote of another absentee Senator who opposes the measure. But almost always there are several Senators who for some reason or other desire to refrain from voting on a particular issue. Under the requirement of a majority of forty-nine Senators for approval, the votes of all such non-voting Senators might just as well be cast in the negative. The requirement for a majority vote of all the Senators, demanded in the Gillette amendment, would put a heavy onus on the supporters of the treaty and would give an unfair advantage to its opponents. It would tend toward minority control, although not in the same degree as the two-thirds rule. The proposal is far from being a liberal improvement of the present system.

The third resolution, which does not have the support of Senator Gillette, admits the House of Representatives to share in treaty-making. But even this resolution retains the objectionable provision requiring a majority of the total membership of both houses for the approval of treaties. A backward step in Senate procedure is proposed in S. J. Res. 52, which seeks to associate the Senate with every step in the negotiation of treaties and at the same time to retain the final consent to ratification in the hands of the Senate. Obviously, this proposal, if adopted, would not only complicate the process of treaty-making, but also would accentuate the troublesome hallucination which pictures the Senate as an executive council of the President.

An adequate amendment will not only abolish the two-thirds rule for ratification but also give the House of Representatives a concurrent share in the consent process. At the same time, it can provide a means for expediting the ratification of the amendment by the several States.

The joint resolution for such an amendment might be couched in the following language:

Resolved by the Senate and the House of Representatives of the United States of America in Congress assembled (two-thirds of each House concurring therein), that the following article is hereby proposed as an amendment to the Constitution of the United States, which shall be valid to all intents and purposes as part of the Constitution when ratified by conventions in three-fourths of the several States:

Section 1. The President shall have power, by and with the advice and consent of Congress, to make treaties provided a majority of the Senators and Representatives present concur.

Section 2. This article shall be inoperative unless it shall have been ratified as an amendment to the Constitution by conventions in the several States as provided in the Constitution, within seven years of the date of the submission thereof to the States by the Congress.

The merits of an amendment of this character are fourfold: (1) It is democratic, for it abolishes the Senate monopoly and confers co-ordinate power on the lower chamber. (2) It abolishes the two-thirds rule. (3) It leaves consent to ratification of treaties in the hands of a majority of the Senators and Representatives present rather than requiring a majority of the total membership of the House and the Senate. This arrangement places legislative action on treaties upon the same basis as the passage of statutory law. (4) By the use of the term "advice and consent," the amendment permits the President to draw Congress into consultation on the negotiation of treaties whenever such assistance is feasible and desirable.

The second section of the proposed amendment is not important. Some legislators hold that there should be some provision for nullifying all ratifications by the States in case the proposed amendment is not approved by three-fourths of the States within a reasonable period of time. They point to the fact that in 1869, the legislature of Ohio solemnly ratified an amendment which had been submitted to it eighty years before that date. Unquestionably, Congress has power to prescribe a reasonable period for ratification if it so desires. As the Supreme Court has implied in the case of Coleman v. Miller (1939), the court will not seek to impose any limitation upon the right of Congress to determine the adoption of an amendment.

Most amendments to the Constitution have been secured through ratifications by the legislatures in three-fourths of the States. The proposal to refer the amendment to conventions in the several States rather than to the legislatures follows the precedent of the Twenty-first Amendment, which was adopted in 1933 as the law of the land within nine and one-half months of submission to the States. While the use of legislatures for the ratification of amendments is more economical, the convention system brings quicker results. Another advantage is that state conventions, being chosen by the people with sole reference to the issue before the country, serve as a national referendum.

When both reason and experience cry aloud for amendment of the Constitution, why should the American people hesitate? Alas, a multitude of arguments are always advanced against any proposal to secure a constitutional reform in such a direct fashion. This hesitation comes largely from two sources: the majority of citizens who are reluctant to tinker with the fundamental law, and vested interests, which would lose their privileged position as a result of a proposed amendment and are not slow to advance plausible reasons to hoodwink the gullible voter.

Because of their veneration for the Constitution, the American people have come, on occasion, preciously close to constitutional stagnation. At times, they seem to have forgotten that the Founding Fathers looked upon the Constitution of 1787 merely as an experiment in government. The letters of Washington and his colleagues show that they were disappointed with the document adopted by the Philadelphia Convention. After concessions had been made to the small States, the new Union became a travesty of the powerful government proposed by Hamilton, Madison, Pinckney, and James Wilson. Nevertheless, Washington and his colleagues were willing to accept the new Constitution as a workable substitute for the intolerable Articles of Confederation. Naturally, they expected the Constitution to be amended from time to time, although they did not realize how difficult the amending process had been made.

The sane attitude toward the Constitution is illustrated by a speech made in Congress in 1796 by Abraham Baldwin, a member of the Constitutional Convention. In it he said:

It is not to disparage the instrument to say that it had not definitely and with precision absolutely settled everything on which it had spoke. He had sufficient evidence to satisfy his own mind that it was not supposed by the makers of it at the time, but that some subjects were left a little ambiguous and uncertain.

The speaker went on to say, as Washington had advised his countrymen in his Farewell Address, that the Constitution must be amended from time to time as the needs of the people required such changes.

On some of the occasions when efforts have been made to promote the public welfare by political and social reforms, sinister forces have been marshalled against the innovators of progress. For instance, the Child Labor Amendment has been fought by manufacturing interests, whose exploitation of cheap labor in both Southern and Northern States was threatened by the proposal to forbid the employment of children.

The defeat of this amendment remains one of the scandals of American politics.

Big Business today does not appear to oppose the reform of the treaty-making process. The United States Chamber of Commerce, the American Association of Manufacturers, the American Bankers' Association, and other representatives of the business world are more tolerant of internationalism. The only isolationist pressure upon Congress from business interests now comes in the field of the Hull Trade Agreements, and even here the pressure seems to have relaxed somewhat. It would seem that Big Business, just like the common man, has perceived the folly of relying upon the policy of neutrality and appeasement as the means of maintaining American peace, and is willing to try the experiment of co-operation. Almost the only vested interest that blocks constitutional reform of the ratification of treaties is the group of Senators who cling to the prestige of their office. Possibly, professional pacifists (men who earn their living out of pacifist propaganda) can be included in this category.

Of all the rationalizations offered in defense of the present undemocratic procedure of ratification, the argument of the need for secrecy and special caution is the most absurd. It carried much weight in the Philadelphia Convention of 1787, where the thinking was in terms of eighteenth century diplomacy. But Washington, Hamilton, and Madison would be the first to admit the necessity for requiring all organs of government to conform to the needs of the age.

It is true that we have not reached the era of "open

covenants openly arrived at" as visioned by Woodrow Wilson. But the requirement of secrecy in the making of treaties has been grossly exaggerated. Today, even the Senate is too large for the secrecy contemplated by the Founding Fathers. In 1789, the Senate numbered only twenty-two members; on cold days, Senators were wont to draw their chairs around the fireplace for more warmth. Now, the Senate numbers ninety-six members. Can ninety-six men be trusted with a secret any more safely than four hundred and thirty-five (the membership in the House of Representatives)? I doubt it.

Again, it was expected that the Senate actually would *advise* with the President during the course of negotiations. President Washington held that view, and in 1789 actually attempted to meet with the Senate for this purpose. His hostile reception ended these endeavors. Thus arose the precedent for the conduct of negotiations exclusively by the executive, and it has been followed by all Presidents since that day. If the original interpretation of "advice and consent" had been observed, there would be grounds for insisting upon secrecy today. But the revival of the theory that the Senate is an executive council, entitled to consultation at every step of the negotiation of treaties, has little merit. In addition, to associate a body of ninety-six members with every stage of diplomatic negotiation would be laborious, time-consuming, and inefficient.

Equally shallow is the argument that a change in the treaty-making process would mean executive usurpation. To Congress, the President is frequently an usurper. In the time of Washington, he was a would-be king; in the time of Lincoln, a tyrant; in the era of Roosevelt, a dictator. It is true that the separation of powers is one of the fundamental doctrines of the Constitution. The Congress is to watch the President; the President is to watch Congress; and the Supreme Court is to watch both of them.

The separation of the functions of negotiation and consent to ratification of treaties was forced upon the executive in Washington's administration by the reluctance of the Senate to advise with the President at every step of the negotiations. Curiously enough, it was nothing but fear of executive usurpation that led the Senate in 1789 to reject the advice and consent procedure suggested by Washington. Anti-Federalists in the Senate strongly objected to the presence of the Chief Executive within the legislative halls. Some feared that the great personage, admittedly first in war, first in peace, and first in the hearts of his countrymen, would move in the direction of monarchy. At any rate, they wanted him to stay outside the Senate chamber, and were willing to sacrifice the advice and consent procedure in order to attain this end.

The argument of executive usurpation is chiefly raised by Senators who fear the loss of the prerogatives of the upper chamber. It is a weak argument. The Constitution can be amended only through the people. If the Constitution is amended by giving the lower house co-ordinate power with the upper house in the matter of consent to ratification, the usurper of the Senate's power is not the President, but the people.

Again, if there be fear of executive usurpation, who, we may well ask, is the best guardian of the liberties of the people? Is it a minority of the upper house? Or is it the majority of the representatives of all the people? Theory as well as practice indicates that the liberties of the citizen can be safeguarded only by recourse to broad popular control. Genuine advocates of liberty in the Senate should welcome the association of the House of Representatives with the upper chamber in preserving civil liberty against any executive usurpation that might be accomplished through the treaty-making process.

There is much more danger in executive usurpation under the present system of treaty-making than under the participation of both houses, on the same basis as statutory enactment. In order to save his treaties from veto by a Senate minority, the President is under the temptation to put all international acts in the form of executive agreements. In 1905, when a Senate minority blocked ratification of the treaty with the Dominican Republic, President Theodore Roosevelt carried out the terms of the nonratified treaty as an executive agreement. Senators called the President a usurper and a violator of the Constitution. But that is all the good it did them. In 1921, when some Democrats in the Senate threatened to oppose the agreements then under negotiation in the Washington Conference on Limitation of Armaments, President Harding, in turn, threatened to put the doubtful treaties in the form of executive agreements. The revolt in the Senate immediately collapsed.

Resort to executive agreements in order to evade the constitutional limitations on treaty-making is becoming more usual as the years go by. In view of the undemocratic character of the present ratifying process, administrators defend the substitution of executive agreements for treaties; eminent jurists condone the evasion; politicians extol it.

Even so, this practice harbors the germs of usurpation. For if executive agreements be dissociated from joint resolutions of both houses of Congress, the Executive is free to negotiate treaties in the form of executive agreements and put them into effect without any reference to the national legislature. The exigencies of the times might force Presidents into a perpetual neglect of the Senate's constitutional share in treaty-making. A genuine interest in thwarting executive usurpation should lead every Senator to support a constitutional reform that would remove all excuse for the President to ignore the legislative will.

An international specter conjured up to frighten the American voter is the dire prediction of loss of national sovereignty. It is the cheapest argument to use against any improvement in the conduct of foreign policy or any commitment for international co-operation. The argument rests on the assumption that the President will destroy the Constitution, bargain away the sovereignty of the United States, and dissolve our independence in international slavery. It was one of the favorite arguments in the bizarre debates over the Treaty of Versailles.

Read the words of Senator Miles **Poindexter**, of Washington, who said:

There is no other nation which today is more absolutely sovereign than the United States. The question now presented is whether or not this high sovereign jurisdiction of the political heirs of Jefferson, Washington and Lincoln is to be in part surrendered and subjected to the control of strangers and aliens.

Even as good a constitutional lawyer as Senator Philander C. Knox, of Pennsylvania, gave utterance to the following misstatement:

Cast up in your mind the colossal powers granted to the Council of the League of Nations. Be it always remembered, we are but one out of nine participating powers. Recall the far-reaching and vital covenants into which we shall enter as one of the high-contracting parties. And hold in mind that we are to give up the power to say when we shall have war, when peace, what our army shall number, how many vessels of war shall we have, how, when and where, and under what conditions shall our army and navy be used, when shall our treaties be binding, what shall our treatment of commerce be, how great shall our gifts of funds be, and, therefore, how great the tribute we shall pay. Consider all these, and you cannot but say that our sovereignty has in matters of national life and death been destroyed.

These statements were pure buncombe, and undoubtedly Senator Knox knew it. The Covenant did not create a superstate. The League of Nations was entirely within the framework of the states system.

The national independence of every member state was guaranteed by every other member state. The resolutions of the Council of the League, to which the Senator referred, were not orders, decrees, laws, or commands from a superior to an inferior. They were simply recommendations. And no state was under obligation to use its economic, financial, or military resources to enforce the recommendations unless it had voted for them in the Council.

Similar absurdities regarding the loss of sovereignty through international co-operation have been made by isolationist Senators in the debates preceding Pearl Harbor. Doubtless they will be repeated during the negotiations that terminate World War II. It is true, of course, that a President of the United States might enter into engagements that destroyed the sovereignty of this country. To date, no President, not even Woodrow Wilson, has ever negotiated an agreement that in any way impaired our independence. If some Chief Executive in the future should attempt a conquest of power through the negotiation of international agreements, he would be more effectively blocked by the combined strength of the two houses of Congress than by the unassisted efforts of the upper chamber.

As already described, the monopoly of advice and consent to treaties which was granted to the Senate by the Founding Fathers grew out of the practice of the Congress of the Confederation. In that body, every State had an equal voice in the concluding of treaties. In the Constitutional Convention, the small States demanded the continuance of this equality of treaty-making. They won their demand, as they won many other claims advanced in that illustrious convention. Thus, the loose theory known as the States Rights doctrine embraced State sovereignty, equality of States, and an equal voice in advice and consent regarding treaties and federal appointments.

The wisdom of the Founding Fathers in accepting the compromises of 1787 has won the admiration of generations of commentators. Stubborn refusal of such compromises by the large States would have led to civil disturbances of a menacing character. But the compromises of the Philadelphia Convention have not barred the descendants of the Founding Fathers from modifying the original federalism.

A shattering blow was dealt the States Rights doctrine by the Civil War. As the functions of the federal government have expanded, as the doctrines of the new nationalism and of the inherent sovereignty of the national government have captured the imagination of the American people, the constitutional position of the States has been greatly modified. The national supremacy has grown, although not at the expense of local autonomy and liberty. The actual course of American federalism was revealingly explained by Frederick Jackson Turner in the following words: "We in America are really a federation of sections rather than of States. State sovereignty has never been influential except as a constitutional shield for a section. In political matters, the States act as groups rather than as individual members of the Union. They act in sections and are responsible to the respective interests and ideals of these sections."

States today are no longer what they were in 1787. In the words of Charles E. Merriam: "Most States do not now correspond to economic or social unities, and their validity as units of organization and representation may be and has been seriously challenged." So far as it concerns foreign policy, the new federalism need not cling to the equality of States in the process of ratification of treaties. The Constitution barred the reduction of equal representation in the Senate of any State, without its consent. But Article V of the Constitution, which provides that no State, without its consent, shall be deprived of its equal suffrage in the Senate, places no other limitation upon the amending power. In other words, the powers of the Senate regarding treaties or any other subject, as well as the powers of the House of Representatives, may be altered by amendment of the Constitution.

Another specious argument is that the liberties of the American people can best be safeguarded by preserving the prerogatives of the Senate. This theory was a favorite during the quarrel between Andrew Jackson and the Senate. It has appeared in the contests of the upper chamber with William Howard Taft, Woodrow Wilson, and the two Roosevelts.

Obviously, the liberties of the people must be preserved. No democratic person would deny that sentiment. Likewise, without question, one of the functions of the legislature is the preservation of personal liberties, as well as the promotion of the general welfare.

But this does not imply that the Senate is more capable of conserving personal liberty than is the House of Representatives. In union there is, indeed, strength. The association of the lower house (representing all the people in equal proportion) with the upper chamber (representing the people in unequal proportion) should give added weight to the guardianship of individual liberty and national independence.

One of the features of the debate on the Covenant of the League of Nations was the demand for the preservation of the prerogatives of the Senate. As if the maintenance of the prestige of the Senate were the only means of safeguarding the liberty of the American people! The same attitude has been apparent on numerous occasions when foreign policy is the subject before the Senate. Already, Senators who oppose constitutional amendment in favor of abolishing the Senate monopoly on ratification have raised the argument of Senatorial prerogatives. Prestige is a dear possession in the eyes of many Senators.

There is something unseemly in the use of this argument by Senators who seek to block a democratic amendment of the treaty-making power. Such Senators give the impression that they believe themselves to have a vested interest in the prerogatives of their office. Admittedly, the adoption of this democratic amendment would somewhat diminish the prestige of Senators. But why should the selfish interest of a few Senators stand in the way of democratic reform?

Senators who oppose the abolition of the Senate's monopoly over ratification of treaties usually end their arguments with the assertion that it is now too late to amend the Constitution. The Peace Treaty for terminating the Second World War, they say, will reach the Senate before the legislatures of three-fourths of the States could ratify the amendment proposed by Congress. They also add, with a touch of satisfaction, that a resolution for an amendment requires the approval of two-thirds of both houses of Congress, and that it is doubtful whether the resolution would command such a high majority in the upper chamber.

This begs the question. As long as government exists, it is never too late to correct its imperfections. Even if the proposed amendment were not adopted before the peace settlement is negotiated, defenders of democracy hope that after the passage of such an amendment, would-be dictators would think twice before provoking a Third World War which, after the correction of American constitutional law, would end in a universal peace treaty acceptable to the American ratifying process. Procrastination in undertaking the task of reforming the antiquated process of treaty-making may impair the leadership of the United States in the counsels of the United Nations. In turn, the inadequacy of our leadership may be one of the many conditions that would inexorably bring on the third global catastrophe of the twentieth century. Regardless of this war or a possible war in the future, however, our treaty-making process is undemocratic, and requires change. Why aspire to democracy unless we practice it in such an important function of government as the making of treaties?

It is erroneous to contend, as was recently done in the Senate, that the amending process cannot be hastened. If public opinion is aroused, the adoption of amendments can proceed with considerable speed. The Twenty-first Amendment (repeal of the Prohibition Amendment) was submitted by Congress to the States on February 20, 1933. Thirty-six ratifications were obtained by December 5, 1933, and the amendment was immediately proclaimed. In other words, the latest amendment to our Constitution was accomplished within nine and one-half months. The Fifteenth, Seventeenth, and Twentieth Amendments were each ratified within one year of proposal.

It would even be possible to secure a decision on ratification of a proposed amendment on a given day previously determined by Congress. For instance, the proposed amendment might provide that ratifying conventions be chosen in all of the forty-eight States to meet in every State capital, say on the Tuesday following the first Monday in the fourth month following the adoption of the joint resolution by Congress.

There is little question as to the constitutionality of this procedure. Congress by resolution can determine that the States must act upon ratification of an amendment by conventions rather than by the legislatures. By the same token, Congress has authority to designate the time of election of the members of the ratifying conventions in the States and the convening of these representative bodies. These facts are not generally known to the American people. If they were better known, the solemn arguments of Senators regarding the slowness that must always be expected of reform by amendment would bear less weight.

One of the assumptions of isolationists in the United States is the claim that international co-operation means the loss of national sovereignty and submission to foreign dictation. It is also assumed that in international collaboration all the sacrifices will be made by the United States and none by other powers. Closely allied with these assumptions is the thesis that in diplomatic conferences the United States has always made the concessions and foreign powers have garnered all the triumphs.

All of these assumptions are false. International co-operation does not entail loss of independence. International collaboration, if correctly executed, will always involve sacrifices by all participants. Finally, in the past century, the United States has won a greater number of important demands at international conferences than any other power. The Paris Peace Conference in 1919 was no exception in this record of diplomatic achievements.

The argument for American participation in international co-operation can even be based on pure self-interest. The reasoning runs as follows: the American people desire peace and prosperity; international co-operation is the only method to banish war, which will aid the promotion of national prosperity; therefore, the United States should participate in international co-operation. This pattern of thinking seems to have been accepted by the American people who are now ready to see their government undertake great commitments for the realization of their peace aims. They are determined, as President Roosevelt has said, not to find themselves in a position where they have won the war only to lose the peace.

But can the American government undertake these commitments under our present treaty-making procedure? Probably not without a continued evasion of the Constitution. In the interest of an orderly constitutional procedure for the negotiation of postwar pacts over a period of many years the Constitution of the United States should be amended so as to bring it into harmony with the needs of twentieth-century diplomacy.

Isolationists and pacifists have insisted that instead of engaging in internationalism, America should perfect democracy at home and thereby set an example for all countries to follow. The challenge of these lame counsels of perfection is accepted. There should be democracy, more democracy, and still more democracy. But let us not forget to include among our democratic reforms at home the correction of our undemocratic procedure in the ratification of treaties. Democracy in this country is deficient as long as foreign policy is at the mercy of a small minority in the oligarchic upper chamber of our national legislature.

Finally, there is a moral issue that must be faced by patriotic Americans. National morality implies the conformity of state action with fundamental principles of justice and public welfare. These principles may slowly evolve as humanity moves down the ages. But the day-to-day position of the state in the stream of multitudinous events requires constant alteration for the purpose of conformity with the fundamental principles. Thus, statecraft requires action, not negation.

In this sense, abstaining from action for fear of making mistakes is one of the most immoral of national policies. Alexander Hamilton roundly condemned the "negative merit of not doing harm, instead of the positive merit of doing good." Such a rule of conduct is slothful, enervating, decadent, character-destroying, and immoral. A do-nothing nation does not serve the best interests of its people.

Action rather than inaction, as a guide to political conduct, applies to international as well as internal politics. Thus, it follows that the negative restriction upon the treaty-making power in the United States is in conflict with the moral code of this forward-looking nation. A great state must not permit itself to be shackled in this undemocratic manner.

The victory of American armed forces in Europe, Africa, and Asia, as well as upon the high seas, may be thrown to the winds if the achievements of the battlefield are not followed up by victories of the peace table. In the matter of constitutional government we are unprepared for effective participation in the management of the United Nations. A democratic amendment of our Constitution is as much needed for winning a permanent peace as the building of armaments to defeat the Axis enemies of democracy.

APPENDIX

BIBLIOGRAPHY

As THE reader is aware, the subject of the amendment of the treaty-making power touches many fields of constitutional law, party politics, public opinion, foreign policy, and diplomacy. In all of these fields exists an extensive literature. A rapid survey of these sources is given in the appendix.

The definitive collection of American treaties is *Treaties and Other International Acts of the United States of America,* edited by Hunter Miller (Publications of the Department of State, Washington, 1931-date). Six volumes have been issued to date, giving the text and critical notes on all treaties from 1776 to 1855. This compilation, when completed, will supersede *Treaties, Conventions, International Acts, Protocols and Agreements between the United States of America and Other Powers* compiled by William M. Malloy (Government Printing Office, Washington, 1910-1923, 3 vols.).

As soon as proclaimed, treaties are published by the Department of State in the *Treaty Series*. Publication of this series began in the year 1929 and continues to date. The *Executive Agreement Series,* initiated in the year 1929, continues to date. Treaties are also published in the *Statutes at Large of the United States, Concurrent Resolutions, Treaties, Conventions and Executive Proclamations* (Washington, 1875-date). This document is usually cited as *U. S. Statutes at Large.* For acts of Congress relating to treaties, see the *United States Code* (1940 edition,

Government Printing Office, Washington, 1941, 4 vols.) and its supplements.

Considerable information regarding the negotiation of treaties and executive agreements is found in the current issues of the *Department of State: Bulletin,* published weekly since 1939. Diplomatic correspondence is published year by year in *Papers Relating to Foreign Relations of the United States, with the Annual Message of the President to Congress* (Washington, 1861-date). The series is usually cited as *U. S. Foreign Relations.* The published correspondence starts with the year 1861. The last volume, published in 1943, comes to the year 1928. This series includes several volumes entitled *The Paris Peace Conference* (Washington, 1942-date) containing stenographic records and other papers of the conference which drafted the peace settlement at the end of World War I. Only four volumes of the contemplated eleven or more volumes have been published.

Further information regarding the negotiation of treaties is to be gleaned from *A Digest of the International Law of the United States,* edited by Francis Wharton (2nd ed., Washington, 1887, 3 vols.). This was followed by *A Digest of International Law,* edited by John Bassett Moore (Government Printing Office, Washington, 1906, 8 vols.). This compilation is expanded by the *Digest of International Law,* edited by Green Haywood Hackworth (Government Printing Office, Washington, 1940-date). Six volumes have been published to date.

The leading treatise on international law as viewed by American authorities is Charles Cheney Hyde, *International Law Chiefly as Interpreted and Applied by American Courts* (Boston, 1922, 2 vols.). The classic treatise is Henry Wheaton, *Elements of International Law,* 2nd ed., edited by William B. Lawrence (Boston, 1863). A competent treatise is Charles G. Fenwick, *International Law* (New York, 1934).

Congressional debates on foreign policy are to be found in the *Congressional Record* (Government Printing Office, Washington, 1874-date). This periodical, issued from day to day while Congress is in session, contains a stenographic record of the debates and proceedings in the Senate and the House of Representatives. The debates in Congress previous to 1874 are to be found in the *Annals of Congress* (1789-1824), the *Register of Debates in Congress* (1824-1837), and the *Congressional Globe* (1834-1874).

Proceedings of the executive sessions of the Senate are to be found in the *Journal of Executive Proceedings of the Senate, First to Fifty-eighth Congress, 1789-1905* (Washington, 1905-date). This set of 39 volumes has not been released to libraries. Attention should be called to the *Compilation of Reports of the Committee on Foreign Relations, United States Senate, 1789-1901*, edited by Hawkin Taylor (Washington, 1901, 8 vols.).

For official commentaries on the treaty-making power, see *The Constitution of the United States: Annotated* (Government Printing Office, 1938). This is Senate Document No. 232, Seventy-fourth Congress, 2nd session. See also the privately published *United States Code Annotated* (West Publishing Company, St. Paul, 1927-date, 82 vols.).

The principal documents regarding the Constitutional Convention which met in Philadelphia in 1787 have been published in convenient form in *The Records of the Federal Convention of 1787*, edited by Max Farrand (Yale University Press, New Haven, 1911, 3 vols.). Various other papers have been printed in *Documents Illustrative of the Formation of the Union of the American States* (House

Document No. 389, Sixty-ninth Congress, 2nd session, Washington, 1927). Both of these collections contain the text of Madison's renowned Journal of the Constitutional Convention. The proceedings of the ratifying conventions are published in *The Debates in the Several State Conventions on the Adoption of the Federal Constitution as Recommended by the General Convention at Philadelphia in 1787*, edited by Jonathan Elliot (Philadelphia, 1836, 5 vols.). Much contemporary information about the Constitutional Convention is found in Charles Warren, *The Making of the Constitution* (Boston, 1929). Material upon the Founding Fathers can be gleaned from their papers. See *The Writings of George Washington*, edited by Worthington Chauncey Ford (New York, 1889-1893, 14 vols.) ; *The Works of Alexander Hamilton*, edited by John C. Hamilton (New York, 1851, 7 vols.); *The Works of James Wilson*, edited by James D. Andrews (Chicago, 1896, 2 vols.) . An excellent edition of Madison's Journal of the Constitutional Convention is found in Vols. III and IV of *The Writings of James Madison*, edited by Gaillard Hunt (New York, 1900-1910, 9 vols.). John Adams was the American minister to England and Thomas Jefferson minister to France when the Constitutional Convention of 1787 met; nevertheless their works must be consulted for origins of American constitutional theory and practice. See *The Works of John Adams*, edited by Charles Francis Adams (Boston, 1856, 10 vols.); and *The Writings of Thomas Jefferson*, edited by Paul Leicester Ford (New York, 1892-1899, 10 vols.).

The first edition of *The Federalist*, the collection of essays written by Alexander Hamilton, James Madison, and John Jay, and printed in New York newspapers in 1787-1788, was published by J. and A. McLean under the title

The Federalist: A Collection of Essays, Written in Favour of the New Constitution, as Agreed upon by the Federal Convention, September 17, 1787 (New York, 1788, 2 vols.). A convenient one-volume edition is that edited by Henry Cabot Lodge and Charles W. Pierson and published in New York in 1888.

Regarding proposals to amend the Constitution, see *The Proposed Amendments to the Constitution of the United States during the First Century of its History* by Herman V. Ames in the *Annual Report of the American Historical Association, 1896* (Washington, 1897, 2 vols.). The list of proposed amendments compiled by Ames stops at the year 1889. A continuation of this list appears in *Proposed Amendments to the Constitution of the United States Introduced in Congress from December 4, 1889 to July 2, 1926* (Senate Document No. 93, Sixty-ninth Congress, 1st session, 1926). A further list is found in *Proposed Amendments to the Constitution of the United States Introduced in Congress from December 6, 1926 to January 2, 1941* (Government Printing Office, Washington, 1941). A discussion of the amending technique is found in Denys P. Myers, *The Process of Constitutional Amendment* (Senate Document No. 314, Seventy-sixth Congress, 3rd session, Washington, 1940).

The standard treatises on American constitutional law contain commentaries on the treaty-making power. See Westel W. Willoughby, *The Constitutional Law of the United States* (2nd ed., New York, 1929, 3 vols.). A classic among treatises is that of Joseph Story, *Commentaries on the Constitution of the United States* (Boston, 1839, 2 vols.). See also Thomas M. Cooley, *A Treatise on Constitutional Limitations,* 8th ed., edited by Walter Carrington (Boston, 1927, 2 vols.). Among the commentaries on treaty law, see Charles H. Butler, *The Treaty-Making Power of the United States* (New York, 1902).

One of the most scholarly books in the field of international acts is by Wallace McClure, *International Executive Agreements: Democratic Procedure under the Constitution of the United States* (New York, 1941) . The book presents a cogent argument in favor of substituting executive agreements for treaties because of the undemocratic character of the American treaty-making process. An outstanding treatise is that of Quincy Wright, *The Control of American Foreign Relations* (New York, 1922). See also John M. Mathews, *American Foreign Relations: Conduct and Policies* (New York, 1938).

A revealing survey of the President's authority in foreign relations is given by Edward S. Corwin, *The President: Office and Powers* (New York, 1941). In his *The President's Control of Foreign Relations* (Princeton, 1917) , Professor Corwin has reviewed classic controversies over the treaty-making power.

Standard treatises on treaty-making are Samuel B. Crandall, *Treaties: Their Making and Enforcement* (2nd ed., Washington, 1916); Arnold Duncan McNair, *The Law of Treaties: British Practice and Opinions* (New York, 1938); Ralph Arnold, *Treaty-Making Procedure* (London, 1933); and Francis O. Wilcox, *The Ratification of International Conventions* (London, 1935). Considerable primary material on the ratification of treaties is contained in *Ratification of Treaties* (Senate Document No. 26, Sixty-sixth Congress, 2nd session, Washington, 1919).

The pioneer work on Senate behavior in treaty-making is that of Joseph Ralston Hayden, entitled *The Senate and Treaties, 1789-1817* (New York, 1920) . An outstanding contribution was made by Denna Frank Fleming in his

The Treaty Veto of the American Senate (New York, 1930). See also his *The United States and the League of Nations, 1918-20* (New York, 1932). An illuminating study of partisanship in treaty-wrecking is Clarence A. Berdahl, *Policy of the United States and the League of Nations* (Geneva, 1945). Another scholarly work giving special attention to the struggle over the Treaty of Versailles is W. Stull Holt, *Treaties Defeated by the Senate* (Baltimore, 1933). What can be said in extenuation of the Senate is written in Royden J. Dangerfield, *In Defense of the Senate: A Study in Treaty-Making* (Oklahoma, 1933).

A history of the organization of the Department of State is given by Gaillard Hunt, *The Department of State of the United States: Its History and Functions* (New Haven, 1914). Among more recent books are Bertram D. Hulen, *Inside the Department of State* (New York, 1939); and Graham H. Stuart, *American Diplomatic and Consular Practice* (New York, 1936). A caustic criticism of the personnel of the Department of State is found in Robert Bendiner, *The Riddle of the State Department* (New York, 1942). The organization and regulations of the Department of State are briefly set forth in the *Department of State of the United States* (Washington, 1941). See also the *United States Government Manual*, published three times a year by the Office of War Information. The personnel of the Department is listed in *Register of the Department of State* (Washington, 1869-date).

The leading treatise on the Senate is George H. Haynes, *The Senate of the United States* (Boston, 1938, 2 vols.). See also Lindsay Rogers, *The American Senate* (New York, 1926); Franklin L. Burdette, *Filibustering in the Senate* (Princeton, 1940); and Roland Young, *This is Congress* (New York, 1943). A history of the Committee on

Foreign Relations in the Senate is found in Eleanor E. Dennison, *The Senate Foreign Relations Committee* (Stanford University, 1942).

An eye-witness account of the celebrated meeting of George Washington with the Senate in 1789 is given in the *Journal of William Maclay: United States Senator from Pennsylvania, 1789-1791,* edited by Edgar S. Maclay (New York, 1890). A verbatim account of the meeting of President Wilson with the Senate Committee on Foreign Relations is recorded in *Treaty of Peace with Germany: Hearings before the Committee on Foreign Relations, United States Senate* (Sixty-sixth Congress, 2nd session, Washington, 1919).

Accounts of senatorial behavior in the international crisis of 1935-1941 include: Joseph Alsop and Robert Kintner, *American White Paper* (New York, 1940); Forrest Davis and Ernest K. Lindley, *How War Came* (New York, 1942); Marquis W. Childs, *I Write from Washington* (New York, 1942); and Rex Stout, *The Illustrious Dunderheads* (New York, 1942).

The memoirs and biographies of the Presidents, Secretaries of State, Senators and diplomats contain revealing pages. Short biographies of the Secretaries of State are contained in the series entitled *The American Secretaries of State and Their Diplomacy,* edited by Samuel F. Bemis (New York, 1927-1929, 10 vols.).

The *Memoirs of John Quincy Adams,* edited by Charles Francis Adams (Philadelphia, 1874-1877, 12 vols.) give Adams' account of the defeat of the Slave Trade Treaty of 1824. See also *Life and Correspondence of Rufus King,* edited by Charles R. King (New York, 1894-1900, 6 vols.); and the *Autobiography of Martin Van Buren.*

The defeat of the Johnson-Clarendon Treaty of 1869 as

told in memoirs is found in Frederick W. Seward, *Autobiography of William H. Seward* (New York, 1877-1891, 3 vols.); *Memoirs and Letters of Charles Sumner,* edited by E. L. Pierce (Boston, 1877-1893, 4 vols.); Bernard C. Steiner, *The Life of Reverdy Johnson* (Baltimore, 1914).

The Senate obstruction of the treaty of 1897 for the annexation of Hawaii is told in the *Diplomatic Memoirs of John W. Foster* (New York, 1909, 2 vols.). See also his *American Diplomacy in the Orient* (Boston, 1904). *The Reminiscences of Carl Schurz* (New York, 1908, 3 vols.) are revealing.

The standard biography of John Hay is Tyler Dennett, *John Hay: From Poetry to Politics* (New York, 1934). An earlier work by William Roscoe Thayer, *The Life and Letters of John Hay* (Boston, 1908, 2 vols.) appears to have been approved by Theodore Roosevelt. In 1908, Mrs. Hay had printed a small edition of *Letters of John Hay and Extracts from Diary.* The spirit of Hay is well shown in the classic *The Education of Henry Adams* (Boston, 1918). See also Alfred L. P. Dennis, *Adventures in American Diplomacy, 1896-1906* (New York, 1928).

A very frank discussion of his relations with the Senate in the matter of foreign policy is told by Theodore Roosevelt in his *Theodore Roosevelt: An Autobiography* (New York, 1919). See also Joseph B. Bishop, *Theodore Roosevelt and His Time* (New York, 1920, 2 vols.); Henry F. Pringle, *Theodore Roosevelt: A Biography* (New York, 1931); as well as *Selections from the Correspondence of Theodore Roosevelt and Henry Cabot Lodge, 1884-1918* (New York, 1925, 2 vols.). Notable information regarding his service as Secretary of State is to be found in the biography of *Elihu Root* by Philip C. Jessup (New York, 1938, 2 vols.). The best biography of Taft is Henry F. Pringle,

The Life and Letters of William Howard Taft (New York, 1939, 2 vols.).

The definitive biography of Woodrow Wilson is written by Ray Stannard Baker under the title *Woodrow Wilson: Life and Letters* (New York, 1927-1939, 8 vols.). The biography ends with the year 1918. The story of Wilson at the Paris Peace Conference is told by Baker in *Woodrow Wilson and World Settlement* (New York, 1923, 3 vols.). These volumes are replete with letters and other documents. See also Edith Bolling Wilson, *My Memoir* (Indianapolis, 1938).

Among other memoirs and biographies of the period of the Paris Peace Conference of 1919 should be cited *The Intimate Papers of Colonel House,* edited by Charles Seymour (Boston, 1926-1928, 4 vols.); and Allan Nevins, *Henry White: Thirty Years of American Diplomacy* (New York, 1930). Primary evidence on the struggle over the Treaty of Versailles in the United States Senate is found in various memoirs and biographies. Henry Cabot Lodge wrote his own defense in *The Senate and the League of Nations* (New York, 1925). Significant memoirs and biographies are *As I Knew Them: Memoirs of James E. Watson* (Indianapolis, 1936); Claude G. Bowers, *Beveridge and the Progressive Era* (Boston, 1932); David Bryn-Jones, *Frank B. Kellogg: A Biography* (New York, 1937).

The documentary side of Franklin D. Roosevelt's treaty-making policy can be followed partly in *The Public Papers and Addresses of Franklin D. Roosevelt* (New York, 1941, 10 vols.). Revealing accounts of the making of foreign policy are given in Forrest Davis and Ernest K. Lindley, *How War Came* (New York, 1942); Joseph Alsop and Robert Kintner, *American White Paper: The Story of Ameri-*

can Diplomacy and the Second World War (New York, 1940).

For a comparison of the parliamentary and the presidential forms of government, see James Bryce, *The American Commonwealth* (4th ed., New York, 1920, 2 vols.); Woodrow Wilson, *Congressional Government* (Boston, 1885) and his *Constitutional Government* (New York, 1908); Charles Grove Haines, *Principles and Problems of Government* (New York, 1934); Henry Hazlitt, *A New Constitution Now* (New York, 1942).

On the subject of public opinion surveys, see George Gallup and Saul F. Rae, *The Pulse of Democracy: The Public Opinion Poll and How It Works* (New York, 1940). The records of polls of the Institute of Public Opinion and the *Fortune Survey* are published from time to time in the *Public Opinion Quarterly*, published by the School of Public Affairs of Princeton University.

RECORDS OF ISOLATIONIST SENATORS

GEORGE D. AIKEN (Vermont, Republican). *Voted against the Administration's attempt to stop Hitler on:* Limit Armed Forces to Western Hemisphere; Two Billion Loan versus Lend Lease Bill; Lend-Lease Bill; Transfer of Axis Ships; Belligerent Zone Restrictions; Armed Ship Bill; Ship Seizure Bill; Second Lend-Lease Bill. *Voted for the Administration's attempt to stop Hitler on:* None.

HUGH A. BUTLER (Nebraska, Republican). *Voted against the Administration's attempt to stop Hitler on:* Limit Armed Forces to Western Hemisphere; Two Billion Loan versus Lend-Lease; Lend-Lease Bill; Transfer of Axis Ships; Extension of the Draft; Belligerent Zone Restrictions; **Armed Ship Bill; Ship Seizure Bill; Second Lend-Lease Bill.** *Voted for the Administration's attempt to stop Hitler on:* None.

C. WAYLAND BROOKS (Illinois, Republican). *Voted against the Administration's attempt to stop Hitler on:* **Limit Armed Forces to Western Hemisphere; Two Billion Loan versus Lend-Lease; Lend-Lease Bill; Transfer of Axis Ships; Extension of the Draft; Belligerent Zone Re-** strictions; Armed Ship Bill; Ship Seizure Bill. *Voted for the Administration's attempt to stop Hitler on:* Second Lend-Lease Bill.

WILLIAM J. BULOW (South Dakota, Democrat. Died in 1942. Succeeded by Harlan J. Bushfield, Republican, also an isolationist). *Voted against the Administration's attempt to stop Hitler on:* Neutrality Revision; Selective Training and Service Bill; Limit Armed Forces to Western Hemisphere; Two Billion Loan versus Lend-Lease; Lend-Lease Bill; Transfer of Axis Ships; Armed Ship Bill; Ship Seizure Bill. *Voted for the Administration's attempt to stop Hitler:* Belligerent Zone Restrictions.

ARTHUR CAPPER (Kansas, Republican). *Voted against the Administration's attempt to stop Hitler on:* Neutrality Revision; Selective Training and Service Bill; Limit Armed Forces to Western Hemisphere; Two Billion Loan versus Lend-Lease; Lend-Lease Bill; Transfer of Axis Ships; Extension of the Draft; Belligerent Zone Re- strictions; Armed Ship Bill; Ship Seizure Bill. *Voted for the Administration's attempt to stop Hitler on:* Second Lend-Lease Bill.

BENNETT CHAMP CLARK (Missouri, Democrat). *Voted against the Administration's attempt to stop Hitler on:* Neutrality Revision; Selective Training and Service Bill; Limit Armed Forces to Western Hemisphere; Two

Billion Loan versus Lend-Lease; Lend-Lease Bill; Transfer of Axis Ships; Extension of the Draft; Belligerent Zone Restrictions; Armed Ship Bill; Ship Seizure Bill; Second Lend-Lease Bill. *Voted for the Administration's attempt to stop Hitler on:* None.

D. WORTH CLARK (Idaho, Democrat). *Voted against the Administration's attempt to stop Hitler on:* Neutrality Revision; Selective Training and Service Bill; Lend-Lease Bill; Transfer of Axis Ships; Extension of the Draft; Belligerent Zone Restrictions; Armed Ship Bill; Ship Seizure Bill; Second Lend-Lease Bill. *Voted for the Administration's attempt to stop Hitler on:* Limit Armed Forces to the Western Hemisphere; Two Billion Loan versus Lend-Lease.

JOHN A. DANAHER (Connecticut, Republican). *Voted against the Administration's attempt to stop Hitler on:* Neutrality Revision; Selective Training and Service Bill; Limit Armed Forces to Western Hemisphere; Two Billion Loan versus Lend-Lease; Lend-Lease Bill; Transfer of Axis Ships; Extension of the Draft; Armed Ship Bill; Ship Seizure Bill; Second Lend-Lease Bill. *Voted for the Administration's attempt to stop Hitler on:* Belligerent Zone Restrictions.

JAMES J. DAVIS (Pennsylvania, Republican). *Voted against the Administration's attempt to stop Hitler on:* Neutrality Revision; Limit Armed Forces to Western Hemisphere; Two Billion Loan versus Lend-Lease; Lend-Lease Bill; Transfer of Axis Ships; Extension of the Draft; Belligerent Zone Restrictions. *Voted for the Administration's attempt to stop Hitler on:* Ship Seizure Bill; Second Lend-Lease Bill.

RUFUS C. HOLMAN (Oregon, Republican). *Voted against the Administration's attempt to stop Hitler on:*

Neutrality Revision; Limit Armed Forces to Western Hemisphere; Two Billion Loan versus Lend-Lease; Lend-Lease Bill; Transfer of Axis Ships; Belligerent Zone Restrictions; Armed Ship Bill; Ship Seizure Bill. *Voted for the Administration's attempt to stop Hitler on:* Second Lend-Lease Bill.

HIRAM W. JOHNSON (California, Republican). *Voted against the Administration's attempt to stop Hitler on:* Neutrality Revision; Selective Training and Service Bill; Limit Armed Forces to Western Hemisphere; Two Billion Loan versus Lend-Lease; Lend-Lease Bill; Transfer of Axis Ships; Extension of the Draft; Belligerent Zone Restrictions; Armed Ship Bill; Ship Seizure Bill; Second Lend-Lease Bill. *Voted for the Administration's attempt to stop Hitler on:* None.

EDWIN C. JOHNSON (Colorado, Democrat). *Voted against the Administration's attempt to stop Hitler on:* Selective Training and Service Bill; Limit Armed Forces to Western Hemisphere; Two Billion Loan versus Lend-Lease; Lend-Lease Bill; Transfer of Axis Ships; Extension of the Draft; Belligerent Zone Restrictions; Armed Ship Bill. *Voted for the Administration's attempt to stop Hitler on:* Neutrality Revision; Ship Seizure Bill.

ROBERT M. LA FOLLETTE (Wisconsin, Progressive). *Voted against the Administration's attempt to stop Hitler on:* Neutrality Revision; Selective Training and Service Bill; Limit Armed Forces to Western Hemisphere; Lend-Lease Bill; Transfer of Axis Ships; Extension of the Draft; Belligerent Zone Restrictions; Armed Ship Bill; Ship Seizure Bill; Second Lend-Lease Bill. *Voted for the Administration's attempt to stop Hitler on:* Two Billion Loan versus Lend-Lease.

WILLIAM LANGER (North Dakota, Republican). *Voted against the Administration's attempt to stop Hitler on:* Neutrality Revision; Selective Training and Service Bill; Limit Armed Forces to the Western Hemisphere; Lend-Lease Bill; Transfer of Axis Ships; Extension of the Draft; Belligerent Zone Restrictions; Armed Ship Bill; Ship Seizure Bill. *Voted for the Administration's attempt to stop Hitler on:* Two Billion Loan versus Lend-Lease.

PAT McCARRAN (Nevada, Democrat). *Voted against the Administration's attempt to stop Hitler on:* Neutrality Revision; Selective Training and Service Bill; Limit Armed Forces to Western Hemisphere; Two Billion Loan versus Lend-Lease; Lend-Lease Bill; Transfer of Axis Ships; Extension of the Draft; Belligerent Zone Restrictions; Armed Ship Bill. *Voted for the Administration's attempt to stop Hitler on:* Ship Seizure Bill.

GERALD P. NYE (North Dakota, Republican). *Voted against the Administration's attempt to stop Hitler on:* Neutrality Revision; Selective Training and Service Bill; Limit Armed Forces to Western Hemisphere; Lend-Lease Bill; Transfer of Axis Ships; Extension of the Draft; Belligerent Zone Restrictions; Armed Ship Bill; Ship Seizure Bill; Second Lend-Lease Bill. *Voted for the Administration's attempt to stop Hitler on:* Two Billion Loan versus Lend-Lease.

ROBERT R. REYNOLDS (North Carolina, Democrat). *Voted against the Administration's attempt to stop Hitler on:* Neutrality Revision; Limit Armed Forces to Western Hemisphere; Lend-Lease Bill; Transfer of Axis Ships; Extension of the Draft; Armed Ship Bill; Second Lend-Lease Bill. *Voted for the Administration's attempt to stop Hitler on:* Selective Training and Service Bill; Ship Seizure Bill.

HENRIK SHIPSTEAD (Minnesota, Republican). *Voted against the Administration's attempt to stop Hitler on:* Neutrality Revision; Selective Training and Service Bill; Limit Armed Forces to Western Hemisphere; Two Billion Loan versus Lend-Lease; Lend-Lease Bill; Transfer of Axis Ships; Extension of the Draft; Belligerent Zone Restrictions; Armed Ship Bill; Ship Seizure Bill; Second Lend-Lease Bill. *Voted for the Administration's attempt to stop Hitler on:* None.

ROBERT A. TAFT (Ohio, Republican). *Voted against the Administration's attempt to stop Hitler on:* Neutrality Revision; Selective Training and Service Bill; Limit Armed Forces to Western Hemisphere; Two Billion Loan versus Lend-Lease; Lend-Lease Bill; Transfer of Axis Ships; Extension of the Draft; Belligerent Zone Restrictions; Armed Ship Bill; Ship Seizure Bill; Second Lend-Lease Bill. *Voted for the Administration's attempt to stop Hitler on:* None.

JOHN THOMAS (Idaho, Republican). *Voted against the Administration's attempt to stop Hitler on:* Limit Armed Forces to Western Hemisphere; Two Billion Loan versus Lend-Lease; Lend-Lease Bill; Transfer of Axis Ships; Extension of the Draft; Belligerent Zone Restrictions; Armed Ship Bill. *Voted for the Administration's attempt to stop Hitler on:* Second Lend-Lease Bill.

CHARLES W. TOBEY (New Hampshire, Republican). *Voted against the Administration's attempt to stop Hitler on:* Neutrality Revision; Limit Armed Forces to Western Hemisphere; Two Billion Loan versus Lend-Lease; Lend-Lease Bill; Transfer of Axis Ships; Extension of the Draft; Belligerent Zone Restrictions; Armed Ship Bill; Ship Seizure Bill. *Voted for the Administration's attempt to stop Hitler on:* Selective Service and Training Bill.

ARTHUR H. VANDENBERG (Michigan, Republican). *Voted against the Administration's attempt to stop Hitler on:* Neutrality Revision; Selective Training and Service Bill; Limit Armed Forces to Western Hemisphere; Two Billion Loan versus Lend-Lease; Lend-Lease Bill; Transfer of Axis Ships; Extension of the Draft; Belligerent Zone Restrictions; Ship Seizure Bill; Second Lend-Lease Bill. *Voted for the Administration's attempt to stop Hitler on:* Armed Ship Bill.

DAVID I. WALSH (Massachusetts, Democrat). *Voted against the Administration's attempt to stop Hitler on:* Neutrality Revision; Selective Training and Service Bill; Limit Armed Forces to Western Hemisphere; Lend-Lease Bill; Transfer of Axis Ships; Extension of the Draft; Belligerent Zone Restrictions; Armed Ship Bill; Second Lend-Lease Bill. *Voted for the Administration's attempt to stop Hitler on:* Two Billion Loan versus Lend-Lease.

BURTON K. WHEELER (Montana, Democrat). *Voted against the Administration's attempt to stop Hitler on:* Neutrality Revision; Selective Training and Service Bill; Limit Armed Forces to Western Hemisphere; Two Billion Loan versus Lend-Lease; Lend-Lease Bill; Transfer of Axis Ships; Extension of the Draft; Belligerent Zone Restrictions; Armed Ship Bill; Ship Seizure Bill; Second Lend-Lease Bill. *Voted for the Administration's attempt to stop Hitler on:* None.

ALEXANDER WILEY (Wisconsin, Republican). *Voted against the Administration's attempt to stop Hitler on:* Neutrality Revision; Selective Training and Service Bill; Limit Armed Forces to Western Hemisphere; Two Billion Loan versus Lend-Lease; Lend-Lease Bill; Transfer of Axis Ships; Extension of the Draft; Belligerent Zone Restrictions; Armed Ship Bill; Ship Seizure Bill; Second

Lend-Lease Bill. *Voted for the Administration's attempt to stop Hitler on:* None.

RAYMOND E. WILLIS (Indiana, Republican). *Voted against the Administration's attempt to stop Hitler on:* Limit Armed Forces to Western Hemisphere; Two Billion Loan versus Lend-Lease; Lend-Lease Bill; Transfer of Axis Ships; Extension of the Draft; Belligerent Zone Restrictions; Armed Ship Bill; Ship Seizure Bill. *Voted for the Administration's attempt to stop Hitler on:* None.

McClurg 2-3-44